And The People Cried, 'Give Us A King!'

". . . they have not rejected you, but they have rejected Me. . ."

"I will lift up mine eyes unto the hills from whence cometh my help. My help comes from the Lord who made heaven and earth"

(Psalms 121:1, 2)

www.thewilltosucceed.homestead.com

And The People Cried, 'Give Us A King!'

ISBN-13: 978-1477472033

We want to hear from you. Please visit us at our website, **www.pomitaly.homestead.com**, or Email us at **pom_ministry@yahoo.com**

More books by James Langston are available at *Amazon,* *Barnes and Nobel, Kindle e-Book, Lulu Incorporated* and *NOOK Books*

Publisher's Cataloging in Publication

Langston, James G., 1958 – As our economy tumbles toward a recession, a cry of change echoes throughout the land. Yet, will this change (a new king) right the wrongs and quell the fears of a troubled, anguished and confused society?

Ordering Information:

Quantity sales/Orders by U.S. trade bookstores and wholesalers. Special discounts are available on quantity purchases by corporations, associations, and others. For details, contact the author.

JAMES LANGSTON
james.langston76@gmail.com

Printed in the United States of America

CONTENTS

Chapter I - <u>21</u>

Make us a King to Judge us
like all the Nations

Chapter II – <u>33</u>

He will take your Sons, for Himself

Chapter III – <u>45</u>

They shall Ear his Ground, Reap his Harvest,
make his Instruments of War,
and Instruments of his Chariots

Chapter IV – <u>55</u>

Your Daughters shall be Confectionaries,
Cooks, and Bakers

Chapter V – <u>67</u>

He will take your Fields,

your Vineyards, your Olive Yards,

and give them to his Servants

Chapter VI – <u>81</u>

He will take the tenth of your Seed,

Sheep and Vineyards,

and give to his Officers, and to his Servants

Chapter VII – <u>91</u>

He will take your Menservants,

Maidservants, your Young Men,

and your Asses, to his Work

Chapter VIII – <u>101</u>

And ye shall cry out because of your King,

and the Lord will not hear you in that Day

Chapter IX – <u>111</u>

Nevertheless, the People refused

to obey the voice of Samuel

Democratic and Republicans
Campaigns of 2008

(a behind the scenes glimpse)

Before the Democratic primaries began, the dichotomy of change versus experience had already become a common theme in the presidential campaign, with Senator Hillary Clinton positioning herself as the candidate with experience and Obama embracing the characterization as the candidate most able to bring change to Washington.

Before the official launch of her campaign, aides for Clinton were already planning to position her as the 'change' candidate, as strategist Mark Penn made clear in an October 2006 memo titled "The Plan." In his presidential run announcement, Obama framed his candidacy by emphasizing that "Washington must change."

In response to this, Clinton adopted her experience as a major campaign theme. By early and mid-2007, polls regularly found voters identifying Clinton as the more experienced candidate and Obama as the "fresh" or "new" candidate.

Exit polls on Super Tuesday found that Obama won voters who thought that the ability to bring change was the most important quality in a candidate, who made up a majority of the Democratic electorate. By a margin of about 2-1, Clinton was able to make up for this deficiency by an almost total domination among voters who thought experience was the most important quality. These margins generally remained the same until Obama clinched the Democratic nomination on June 3.

Obama campaigning as a symbol of change in Cleveland, Ohio with a "Change We Need" sign

Obama's promised "universal health care, full employment, a green America, and an America respected instead of feared by its enemies".

He used new media to "form a bond with his supporters" which helped him "appeal to the youth audience's need to feel special, in-the-know, empowered and special". This was best displayed in his text message announcement of Joe Biden as the vice-presidential candidate.

He has also declared, in his book *The Audacity of Hope*, that he did not experience a religious upbringing. Rather he developed his faith due to the church's ability to motivate social change. Bowdern wrote, "This is best exemplified in his "50 state strategy", where he campaigned in states that historically would never vote for a Democrat. The 2008 presidential election saw a large youth turn out, up to 51 percent."

John McCain quickly adopted similar campaign themes against Obama at the start of the general election campaign. Polls regularly found the general electorate as a whole divided more evenly between 'change' and 'experience' as candidate qualities than the Democratic primary electorate, which split in favor of 'change' by a nearly 2-1 margin.

Advantages for McCain and Obama on experience and the ability to bring change, respectively, remained steady through the November 4 election. However, final pre-election polling found that voters considered Obama's inexperience less of an impediment than McCain's association with sitting President George W. Bush, an association which was rhetorically framed by the Obama campaign throughout the election season as "more of the same".

McCain appeared to undercut his line of attack by picking first-term Alaska governor Sarah Palin to be his running mate. Palin had been governor only since 2006, and before that had been a council member and mayor of Wasilla. Nonetheless, she excited much of the conservative base of the GOP with her speech at the 2008 Republican National Convention, a group that was initially lukewarm toward McCain's candidacy.

However, media interviews suggested that Palin lacked knowledge on certain key issues, and they cast doubt among many voters about her qualifications to be Vice President or President. Because of Palin's conservative views, there was also concern that she would alienate independents and moderates, two groups that pundits observed McCain would need to win the election. (Wikipedia.org)

Foreword

As I immersed myself in the pages of this book, a dominant, yet familiar Verse of Scripture kept running through my spirit, *"To every thing there is a season [change], and a time to every purpose under the heaven"* (Eccl. 3:1).

James lays this foundational truth in such a way that it gives readers a "ruler" whereby they may objectively, yet, impartially measure their service to and for the Lord. To coin a phrase, "Information, information, information ... you can never have too much."

The truths of life and living are presented in such a practical and well-defined manner that a Christian need only respond with a "yes" or a "no" when asked, "Are you actively lifting up the nail-scarred banner of the Lord or simply biding your time sitting on the fence?"

Also as you read, please take a few moments to consider two trains of thought: "Can I benefit from the authors research, and if so, how?" and "Am I guilty of complaining about life but doing little, if anything to change the things that I can (as many do)?"

Life can so tie any of us up with problem after problem that we essentially become useless for the Lord; yet, there are those in Christendom who choose to remain *misinformed* about what's right and what's wrong in this world: their attitude is, "As long as we remain ignorant, we are not responsible."

This book gave me an unabridged and up close and personal lesson about life. With so much falsity in our world (and even in the Church), we sometimes forget that every individual must seek the Lord regarding his or her particular "borders" in life. Once we do, He [our Heavenly Father] will give us the strength and faith to carry out this mission and mandate He has for our lives.

Today, as never before, people from all walks of life, rich, poor, young and old are clamoring for someone [a King] to make things right. However, there is only one King who can right the wrongs of life, the One and True Constant in the midst of the chaos and uncertainty of life – Jesus Christ!

There remains so much work to do, and we [Christians] are the ones chosen for this seemingly impossible task to, "*. . . go ye into all the world and preach the Gospel . . .*"

The truths in this book are truths that every man, woman, boy and girl needs to hear! Yet, if we do not tell them, these truths will

----

forever remain entombed and hidden.

In nature, every living organism has a leader. However, we have the responsibility to discern if their leadership is toward righteousness or unrighteousness.

In the past 50 years, our nations' economy has run more like a roller coaster ride than as a nation of greatness. And, if we [the church] continue to "sleep" (as we are prone to do) and not let our voices be heard, soon we will not be able to stop or alter this ride.

A quick glance at history warns us that our indecisiveness has not only crippled countless generations, but even now this millennial generation is asking, "What have you learned from your failure?" and "What do you know that I should know?"

Admittedly, the answers are never simple. However, the first step is always the most decisive, "Are we willing to get off the sidelines, reposition ourselves, do our homework [read, pray and watch], honor God, and then get to work!"

It is never too late to make the necessary changes, but we must hurry, the hour draws near.

Larry Morris
Project 10 Challenge
May 2008

Acknowledgements

"And He said unto them, He that hath ears to hear, let him hear" (Mk. 4:9)

As I sat in the quietness of our bedroom, I began to sense that still, yet unmistakable Presence of the Holy Spirit: the same One who in the beginning said, *"Let there be light,"* and it was so. His Words were simple, yet weighted with grave responsibility,

"I have anointed you to write a message, do not delay, nor doubt. It will speak to the hearts of many. Yet, you must hurry, the time is near."

As you read this *message*, I pray I can properly convey the urgency of the hour to you.

We are about to experience a change in our way of life that will be *earth shaking*. Yet, this should not be surprising or unexpected.

We have long boasted how we do not need God in our society, in our schools, in our homes or in our lives. Sadly, the same thing we have so brazenly demanded – CHANGE – will turn out to be a snare unto our souls.

What we have failed to comprehend and embrace as it relates to "times" and "seasons," we shall soon look upon with wide-eyed astonishment.

Yet, before these events occur, just as the Prophet Joel foretold, we shall see a great outpouring of the Lord's Spirit in a way the world has never witnessed!

The nearness of the hour is upon us – we <u>must</u> hurry!

"And it shall come to pass afterward, that I will pour out my spirit upon all flesh; and your sons and your daughters shall prophesy, your old men shall dream dreams, your young men shall see visions: And also upon the servants and upon the handmaids in those days will I pour out my spirit. And I will shew wonders in the heavens and in the earth, blood, and fire, and pillars of smoke. The sun shall be turned into darkness, and the moon into blood, before the great and terrible day of the Lord come." (Joel 2:28-31).

James Langston
Senior Pastor, Pilgrim Outreach Ministries
April 2008

Introduction

Top Headlines

(22 May 2008)

SENATOR BARRACK OBAMA 70 VOTES FROM NOMINATION AFTER OREGON WIN

Obama had 1,961 delegates overall, out of 2,026 needed for the nomination.   Clinton had 1,779 in their marathon race that has shattered voter turnout records in state after state. (Associated Press)

SENATOR EDWARD M. KENNEDY HOME TO PLAN CARE

The 76—year old senator, the last son in a famed political family, was diagnosed with a malignant glioma in his left parietal lobe – which   helps   govern   sensation,   movement   and language – after suffering a seizure in his home Saturday (17 May 2008) morning. (Associated Press)

WORLD OIL TOPS 130/BARREL.

LONDON—Oil prices on Wednesday surged above a record high $130 a barrel on a weakening US dollar and an OPEC statement it would maintain present production, sparking worries about stretched supplies amid strong demand for energy. (Philippine Daily Inquirer)

Daily we find that the oddities and uncertainties of life are becoming more and more infused into our life and living. One can only hope for a ray of sunshine in the midst of this endless cycle of madness, chaos, and unfulfilled promises.

I may be the only one confused, but "Why is the Church silent in these critical times?" Why aren't we preaching pulsating messages of revival, instead of sitting on the fence waiting for the arrival of a new "king?"

Israel of old was a people Jehovah favored, watched over and protected from enemies – both from within and without. Yet, with scorn and disdain, they repeatedly broke His laws, and rejected His Word.

The amazement is not that they fell into an economic, moral, and spiritual mess, but that God was so merciful and longsuffering toward them – as He has been toward us.

And the People Cried, Give Us A King, draws a parallel

----

between Israel's plights as they rejected Yahweh, and the fall from grace of another great nation, our nation, the United States of America.

There is one road and one path for all to follow, the way of the Cross. If that way is ignored or rejected, the resultant woes are not only irreversible, but also inevitable.

"And another angel came out from the altar, which had power over fire; and cried with a loud cry to him that had the sharp sickle, saying, Thrust in thy sharp sickle, and gather the clusters of the vine of the earth; for her grapes are fully ripe."

"And the angel thrust in his sickle into the earth, and gathered the vine of the earth, and cast it into the great winepress of the wrath of God. And the winepress was trodden without the city, and blood came out of the winepress, even unto the horse bridles, by the space of a thousand and six hundred furlongs" (Rev. 14:18-20).

James Langston
Senior Pastor, Pilgrim Outreach Ministries
April 2008

(Chapter I)

Make us a King to Judge us
like all the Nations

"A recession looms at the door—before it arrives; we have an opportunity to improve our minds, bodies, and wallets. Though we may soon be denying ourselves more than pleasures, this is what we're omitting right now"

—Andrew Womack

"In a society of little economic development, universal inactivity accompanies universal poverty. You survive not by struggling against nature, or by increasing production, or by relentless labor; instead you survive by expending as little energy as possible, by striving constantly to achieve a state of immobility"

—Ryszard Kapuscinski

"Few can believe that suffering, especially by others, is in vain. Anything that is disagreeable must surely have beneficial economic effects" **—John Kenneth Galbraith**

As our nation staggers toward an uncertain future, a renewed cry is gathering momentum throughout the land, "change." From the rural life in Buford, Wyoming to the chaotic suburbs of New York, New York, people are unexpectedly uniting over a common foe – debt.

While the brightest minds in the nation are scrambling to combat this ever-growing beast, Ben Bernanke, Federal Reserve Chairman recently slashed a key interest rate by three-fourths of a percentage point, moving aggressively to contain a credit crisis threatening to push the country into a severe recession.

He and his colleagues have now cut the funds rate six times since last September (2007). The reductions have become even more aggressive since January (2008) as the central bank has faced growing turmoil in global financial markets.

President Bush always the optimist continues to insist that his fiscal stimulus proposal will work, however; he adds, "It must be big enough to make a difference in an economy as large and as dynamic as ours."

He goes on to say that, "His proposal must be built on broad-based tax relief that will directly affect economic growth, and not the kind of spending projects that would have no immediate impact on our economy."

Yet, in spite of their efforts, a feeling of unrest and déjà vu is felt throughout the nation, "We've heard it and seen it before," says most Americans.

The following is a look at the accumulated spending habits (debt vs. savings) of our nation.

U.S. National Debt Clock
(Accumulated Debt/Savings)

1. **Borrowed by the General Fund** – $ 18,157,963,233,469†
Income: Income taxes. Outgo: Defense 30%, Interest 19%
2. **Saved by the Social Security Trust** + $ 2,818,024,472,079
Income: FICA Payroll taxes. Outgo: Benefits and disability
3. **Saved by other Gov. Trust Funds** + $ 2,275,614,266,418
Income: FICA and gas taxes. Outgo: Medicare, highways, etc.
4. **Debt Held by the Public (net debt)** $ 13,064,324,494,971

Debt Facts:

- Social Security is $2.7 trillion in the black (Nov 2012). In 2010 it ran a $90 billion surplus.
- Clinton reduced the debt as a percent of GDP.
- G. W. Bush restarted the deficits with tax cuts tilted toward the rich, and then continued with Medicare D, two wars and more.
- Red ink hit a peak rate of $1.1 trillion in 100 days just before Obama was elected.
- Obama's stimulus was only $0.8 trillion.
- Only $1.2 trillion is owed to China (11/2012).

†Note: The astonishing $18 trillion gross national debt is owed by the "General Fund." That's the part funded by our income taxes. Half of that amount funds the military, and other half pays interest on the debt. Fortunately, two huge parts of the budget, Social Security and Medicare, are running huge surpluses. (source: zfacts, 25 June 2015)

Anytime you read this type of information, two questions come to mind: What caused this? and What do we do to fix it?

However, before we push the panic button let us not forget that our nation remains the only true superpower in the world. Although we have a shaky and sometimes tumultuous history, we somehow manage to get things together before the midnight bell tolls.

Nevertheless, we as Israel of old have consistently allowed our ways, our ambitions, and our ideals to circumvent the ways of the Lord – and now our incurred debt [to God] is due and marked as "payable on demand."

The Vietnam War, (1963-1971) cost us **$518 billion**: The Gulf war (1991), although not as costly, still ran up a hefty price tag of **$88 billion**: And the wars in Afghanistan (2001) and Iraq (2003) have cost **$604 billion** to date; and with a monthly cost of **$12+ billion**, there remains no simple resolution to these conflicts in the Middle East (source: USA Today).

Although numerous factors have contributed to our current crisis, the two biggest are; record oil prices and the historic weakness of the U.S. dollar abroad.

As a side note, on Wednesday, 27 Feb 2008, oil and gold hit historic highs while the U.S. dollar sank to a historic low. (Gold prices broke the $1,000 / ounce barrier on 13 Mar 2008.) When combined with other factors including the sub-prime mortgage crisis and the stock market downturn, each separate event has helped to push the US into an economic crisis.

The sub-prime mortgage crisis also has caused panic in financial markets and encouraged investors to take their money out of risky mortgage bonds and shaky equities and put it into commodities as "stores of value." Most of the recent increases in global food prices have been the result of speculation and the collapse in the value of the US dollar.

For the first time in history, many believe that an underlying reason of the economic problems is an environmental sustainability crisis, mostly due to commodities costs rising at their fastest rate in years.

Unprecedented demand from China and India, which has never been seen before in history, has caused the prices of finite resources to soar, as well as their depletion rates to increase. (source: Wikipedia)

Someone once said, "If the U.S. is forced into a state of insolvency, it will forever tilt the financial axis of the world."

Facts:

- The buying power of the dollar abroad is at an all time low.

The Euro currency, introduced in 2002, has surpassed the dollar in spend ability and creditability, (source: Reuters)

- New home sales are at a new 16 year low, (source: Money.cnn)
- Foreclosures are up 65 percent over the same period a year ago, (source: MSNBC.msn)
- In some cases, food prices have almost doubled in the past 2 years. (source: Bureau of Labor Statistics)

Staples	2007	2008	2015
Flour	.34 lb	.42 lb	.52 lb
Ground Beef	2.19 lb	2.33 lb	4.14 lb
Whole Chicken	1.03 lb	1.16 lb	1.48 lb

Commodity	2007	2008	2015
Whole Milk	3.07 lb	3.87 lb	3.38 lb
Butter	3.00 lb	3.00 lb	3.00 lb
Corn	4.25 bu	5.46 bu	5.46 bu
Soybeans	7.61 bu	7.61 bu	7.61 bu
Wheat	4.35 bu	11.21 bu	5.35 bu
White Bread	---------	1.28 lb	1.46 lb
Eggs	---------	2.18 dz	1.96 dz
Apples	---------	1.16 lb	1.30 lb

The average price of gas nationwide is $4.00 a gallon (source: Los Angeles Times). Many experts fear that unless the price of crude oil is brought to a reasonable $70 a barrel (currently $140.00 a barrel) (source: Los Angeles Times), by years end the average price for gas may top $7.00 a gallon. (source: EzineArticles.com)

In November 2008, we will elect a new leader, Senator Barack Obama (Democratic nominee), or Senator John McCain (Republican nominee). Ironically, both in their own words are promising to usher in unparalleled changes.

"Change will not come if we wait for some other person or if we wait for some other time. We are the ones we've been waiting for.

We are the change that we seek," —**Barack Obama**

"I think we finally have a poll without a margin of error ... We have sent a powerful message to Washington: Change is coming," —**John McCain**

Yet, can either bring their campaign promises to fruition? If their failure to agree on ten basic issues is any indication, then the answer is no. (source: "Where I Stand")

	Barack Obama	John McCain
1. Based on the information available at the time of the invasion of Iraq, was it justified?	NO	YES
2. Should Roe vs. Wade be overturned?	NO	YES
3. Should the U.S. expand the State Children's Health Insurance Program (SCHIP)?	YES	NO
4. Has the invasion of Iraq been successful?	NO	YES
5. Should the U.S. set a timetable to withdraw troops from Iraq?	YES	NO
6. Based on the information available now, was the invasion of Iraq justified?	NO	YES
7. Should the U.S. deploy more troops to Iraq?	NO	YES
8. Should abstinence-only sex education be taught in schools?	NO	YES
9. Can the use of torture as an interrogation technique be justified?	NO	YES
10. Should the U.S. military maintain its "Don't ask, don't tell" policy?	NO	YES

The cold reality is after the fanfare, the whistles, and loud speeches, changes will not occur overnight: change is a slow, often painful and monotonous process. Sometimes it takes years before any tangible results are realized. I wonder if we as a nation can patiently wait for what was promised.

In state after state, voter turnout for primary elections are shattering records as young and old come together on a single issue of agreement – change. Yet, even as the cry of change echoes from coast to coast, many of our freedoms are eroding right before our eyes.

George Santayana said, *"Those who cannot learn from history are doomed to repeat it."* If we fail to carefully consider our history and continue to ignore the inherent truths of the Word of God, we too are doomed to repeat our failures and in turn be ill prepared for our future.

(1962) HISTORIC SUPREME COURT DECISION, ENGEL VS. VITALE
Banned prayer and devotional Bible readings in public schools.

(1973) HISTORIC SUPREME COURT DECISION, ROE VS. WADE
According to the Roe decision, most laws against abortion in the United States violated a constitutional right to privacy under the Due Process Clause of the Fourteenth Amendment.

(1976) COURTS ALLOW REMOVAL OF LIFE SUPPORT
Karen Ann Quinlan had been in a coma for over a year before her parents won the right to remove the life support equipment keeping her alive. It took 9 years for her to die afterwards.

(1981) ACQUIRED IMMUNE DEFICIENCY SYNDROME (AIDS) VIRUS DEATH
The first reports of homosexual men dying due to a mysterious

breakdown of the bodies' immunization system. Later it becomes known as Acquired Immune Deficiency Syndrome, a.k.a. AIDS and researchers realize it can strike anyone.

(1999) COLUMBINE TRAGEDY

Two students go on a shooting rampage in Columbine High School in Littleton, Colorado. They kill 12 students, 1 teacher and themselves.

(2003) U.S. BACKED "ROAD MAP" FOR PEACE PROPOSED FOR MIDDLE EAST

In an attempt to restart the stalled Israeli-Palestinian peace process, Israel and the United States resolved to circumvent Palestinian leader Yasir Arafat, whom Israeli prime minister Ariel Sharon called "irrelevant" and an obstacle.

(2007) COURT UPHOLDS BAN ON ABORTION PROCEDURE

The ruling, 5–4, which upholds the Partial-Birth Abortion Ban Act, a federal law passed in 2003, is the first to ban a specific type of abortion procedure.

(2008 NOVEMBER) 44TH PRESIDENT OF THE U.S. ELECTED

Election results will determine who succeeds George Bush Jr. as the next leader of the U.S. (Barack Obama or John McCain)

(2009 JANUARY) 44TH PRESIDENT OF THE U.S. INAUGURATION CEREMONIES

Ceremonial event marking the commencement of a new four-year term of a president of the United States.

(????) RAPTURE OF THE CHURCH

"For the Lord himself shall descend from heaven with a shout, with the voice of the archangel, and with the trump of God: and the dead in Christ shall rise first: Then we which are alive and remain shall be caught up together with them in the clouds, to meet the Lord in the air: and so shall we ever be with the Lord" (I Thess. 4:16, 17).

(????) TRIBULATION PERIOD

"And at that time shall Michael stand up, the great prince which standeth for the children of thy people: and there shall be a time of trouble, such as never was since there was a nation even to that same time: and at that time thy people shall be delivered, every one that shall be found written in the book" (Dan. 12:1).

(????) MILLENNIAL REIGN

"And I saw thrones, and they sat upon them, and judgment was given unto them: and I saw the souls of them that were beheaded for the witness of Jesus, and for the word of God, and which had not worshipped the beast, neither his image, neither had received his mark upon their foreheads, or in their hands; and they lived and reigned with Christ a thousand years. But the rest of the dead lived not again until the thousand years were finished. This is the first resurrection. Blessed and holy is he that hath part in the first resurrection: on such the second death hath no power, but they shall be priests of God and of Christ, and shall reign with him a thousand years" (Rev. 20:4-6).

(????) THE NEW HEAVEN AND NEW EARTH

"And I saw a new heaven and a new earth: for the first heaven and the first earth were passed away; and there was no more sea" (Rev. 21:1).

(Chapter II)

He will take your Sons,
for Himself

In 2006, the world held its breath as rescuers frantically searched for thirteen miners trapped hundreds of feet underground in West Virginia. The likelihood that entire generations of miners were now lost was almost too much for families to cope with or accept.

However, as the hours dragged on and rescuers found only one survivor, families, loved ones and even the most curious had to face a cold and hard truth – death waits for no one. Sadly, a system that was designed to protect them had somehow failed them.

Now, fast forward to 2008; a time where hopes, dreams,

successes and failures also hinge on a poor and flawed system: a system of laws and rules instituted by man, interpreted by man, and in many instances subverted by man, all in the name of "justice."

One noted philosopher said, *"The laws of the land are good and fair, however we are not. We've turned our society into a place where the strong survive and the weak [supposed or presumed] eventually perish."*

As Daniel prophesied, *"...knowledge shall be increased,"* we are witnessing today some of the brightest minds coming out of colleges and universities. However, within the frameworks of these same educational systems, crimes of the most hideous and wicked imaginable are being perpetrated: mass-murder, kidnappings, prostitution, and drug dealings to name a few.

Sadly, these and other atrocities are becoming commonplace in these prestigious, middle and upper class universities.

Under the pretext of, "The way to better one self is through education," we have spent billions to educate our children and society about sex, drugs, alcohol, and cigarettes.

Yet, as these efforts failed, as all efforts of the flesh shall, is it any wonder eleven-year-olds are having babies, four and five year olds are drug runners, ten-year-olds are full-blown drunks and twelve-year olds are dying of cigarette related lung cancer.

We're losing our sons and daughters to a system that is full of empty, half-hearted promises and innuendoes. And, if our history of the past one-hundred years is any indicator, this system will not change, regardless of who's in office.

Joseph Stalin once said, "America is like a healthy body and its resistance is threefold: **its patriotism, its morality and its spiritual life.** If we can undermine these three areas, America will collapse from within." Sadly, those three "pegs" have now hooked, tied and marked us.

Fifty years ago when the name of Jesus was mentioned, it carried a sense of belonging. Today, we more identify with "Reebok," "Nike," and "Adidas," than "Matthew," "Mark," "Luke," and "John."

Dr. Martin Luther King Jr. said, "One of the great liabilities of history is that all too many people fail to remain awake through great periods of social change. Every society has its protectors of status quo and its fraternities of the indifferent who are notorious for sleeping through revolutions."

"Today, our very survival depends on our ability to stay awake, to adjust to new ideas, to remain vigilant and to face the challenge of change."

Sadly, we've allowed ourselves to become part of an ever-growing system that cares more about exploitation [what's in it for me] than what's right. However, as we're clamoring for change, we need to come face-to-face with some hard questions regarding this change, "Will the world be better or worse in ten years because of this?" and if not, "Am I willing to accept responsibility for my inaction when these flawed decisions fail?"

What is so bad about the here and now that makes us long for something else? Is it fear, or simply a disregard for truth?

According to the National Institute of Media and the Family, 92 percent of the children in America age 2-17 play video games. Video games, movies, music and mystical arts and its associated paraphernalia are all big businesses of which the dollars from our youth support and finance.

When the august Supreme Court declared it unconstitutional to pray in schools or publically display the Ten Commandments, they arguably were saying, "We will tell you what to read, what to think and in many instances what to say."

How detrimental has their landmark decision been?

(Excerpted from America's Godly Heritage by David Barton)

- Since 1963, when prayer was taken out of school, unwed birth rates of 15-19 year-olds doubled, and pregnancies for girls 10-14 went up 553% (all under the guise of "Separation of Church and State.")

- Divorce rates from 1963 to 1983 were up 117%. For fifteen years prior to 1963, divorce had been declining.

- Since 1963, single families were up 140%, single families with children were up 160%, and unmarried couples living together went up 353%.

- From 1965, there was a sharp incline of gonorrhea in Students in ages 15-19. Its incline became more apparent since the removal of religious principles from school. Student Sexually

Transmitted Diseases (STD's) went up 228%.

- SAT scores approximate average was 970 points from 1952 to 1963. From 1963 to 1980, scores declined for eighteen consecutive years to drop to a low average of 890 points in 1980.

- In 1974-75, the sharp decline in SAT scores slowed with the advent of private religious schools, which allowed religion in the curriculum. During this time, there were 32 thousand U.S. schools, which accounted for 8.5 million students. Some say that better scores for these students came about as private schools had more money available for a better education for these students. Their statements were investigated and it was found that private schools had, on average, $110.00 per student, whereas public schools had $370.52 per student.

- SAT scores showed that students from the Christian private schools, on average, got 100 points higher, than the Non-Christian schooled students. That put the Christian schooled students back on the par where students were prior to 1963 and the separation of church and state. It was as if no change had occurred. Whereas public schooled student scores continued to declined!

- In 1988 – the number of Academic High Achievers were as follows:

  o 60.8 were from public schools

  o 39.2 were from private schools – This group was 3 times larger than those from the public schools were. Remember too, that private religious schools had 1/3 less money per person and used the same curriculum as the public schools, except the private schools added religion.

- Violent crimes went up 544% since religious principles were removed from schools in 1963.

Thomas Jefferson said, *"Religion is the friend to government because it teaches morals of the heart. This means we are not dealing with murder, instead we deal with the religious morals which say do not hate. When we eliminate hate, there is no murder. The commandment to not lust, stops adultery or rape."*

The more you read about lawyers finding "loopholes" in laws to free the guilty from punishment; it makes you wonder if our society is a democracy (of, for and by the people) or a pre-socialistic state (a political theory advocating state ownership of industry).

We're at a crossroads as a nation and people, and unless we come back to Biblically established rights and wrongs, we will soon find ourselves a byword in the mouth of the world.

Sadly, since the church (as a whole) has failed to preach the Gospel (the truth, the whole truth and nothing but the truth); the world and a growing number of Christians now turn to something or someone else to tell them what they need to know.

Do you realize that 23 percent of the U.S. populate is illiterate? That's one in five Americans lacking the basic reading skills beyond a 4th grade level. Statistics tell us that approximately 39 million people in affluent, pristine, enlightened America cannot read or write! (US government report, The State of Literacy in America, released by the National Institute for Literacy (NIL))

Newspapers, Television, Radio, Internet, political analyst, Hollywood, etc., are now our "trusted" source of information and learning. If these sources had the Word of God as their reference, this would not be tragic, yet sadly, they do not.

Ironically, it's whoever shouts the loudest and most often, that gets our attention, and eventually our vote. How true the adage, "The squeaky wheel gets the grease."

Senators Barack Obama, and John McCain have emphatically made promises of change: changes in our government, our society, and in our war policy in Iraq and Afghanistan. However, we live in a dysfunctional world; a place where what comes out of one side of our mouth doesn't necessarily sound the same when it comes out the other side.

For example, When Barack Obama was asked about meeting with leaders of countries hostile to the United States, including countries such as Cuba and Iran, he said,

"It is time to pursue direct diplomacy, with friend and foe alike, without preconditions. There will be careful preparation. We will set a clear agenda," he said.

"I would be willing to lead that diplomacy at a time and place of my choosing, but only when we have an opportunity to advance the interests of the United States." (Reuters)

And John McCain said, "I promise to cut hundreds of billions of

----

dollars out of wasteful and unnecessary spending in America."

When asked what if Congress does not give him the spending cuts he promises, would he hold off on signing the tax cuts, his response was, "No, of course not." Nonetheless, "We're going to be on a path to a balanced budget." Big spenders, watch out! "I'm their worst nightmare, my friend." (Reuters)

Although both can't be right, they certainly can be wrong. In November of this year, your vote will decide who leads this country for the next 4 years. However, before we look ahead to those elections, let's conjecture for a moment.

What if ... and I say, "What if," with the greatest of caution, what if something so cataclysmic and dynamic occurs in the U.S. that national elections are cancelled. Are you ready for this unexpected change?

"Washington, DC — President Barack Obama shocked the country this morning with news that he is running for a third term.

"I can't abandon the American people now when they need me more than ever," Obama told reporters at a press conference this morning. "We've come this far as a nation, now is not the time to do something different. This is the change you wanted and this is the change you're getting."

Senator Rand Paul of Kentucky told CNN he does not agree with Obama and his announcement. "This defies everything the Constitution stands for," Paul said. "We can not let this man have a third term."

In the history of this country only two presidents have served more than two terms, Theodore Roosevelt and Franklin D. Roosevelt. The major problem for Obama when he runs in 2016, is the 22nd Amendment. In short, the 22nd Amendment states, "No person shall be elected to the office of the President more than twice..." (source: Darious Rubics (News Examiner))

One constant about life is its fluidity. I, as you, would shudder to think of the chaos and pandemonium such an event could bring. Yet, if the unthinkable occurred, President Obama would then enact his "National Security and Homeland Security Presidential Directive."

The directive establishes a comprehensive national policy on the continuity of Federal Government structures and operations and a single National Continuity Coordinator responsible for coordinating the development and implementation of Federal continuity policies.

In other words, a domestic policy for carrying out "National Essential Functions" is immediately established. It further prescribes continuity requirements for all executive departments and agencies, and, provides guidance for State, local, territorial, and tribal governments, and private sector organizations to ensure a comprehensive and integrated national continuity program that will enhance the credibility of our national security posture.

Lastly, it enables a more rapid and effective response to and recovery from a national emergency (National Security Presidential Directive/NSPD-51, Homeland Security Presidential Directive

NSPD-20 dtd 5 May 2007).

I pray these measures are never enacted, for history warns us that once the floodgates are opened, it's often difficult to close them; however, the mechanism for such an event is already in place.

In October of 1962, President John F. Kennedy addressed the nation regarding the recent Cuban Missile Crisis. His speech while relatively short (16 minutes 55 seconds), was filled with words of strength and determination. When Mr. Kennedy concluded his speech, Russian Premier Nikita Khrushchev knew he [President Kennedy] was prepared to do "whatever it took," to ensure America's peaceful way of life was not jeopardized.

"This Nation is prepared to present its case against the Soviet threat to peace, and our own proposals for a peaceful world, at any time and in any forum--in the Organization of American States (OAS), in the United Nations, or in any other meeting that could be useful--without limiting our freedom of action. We have in the past made strenuous efforts to limit the spread of nuclear weapons."

"We have proposed the elimination of all arms and military bases in a fair and effective disarmament treaty. We are prepared to discuss new proposals for the removal of tensions on both sides – including the possibility of a genuinely independent Cuba, free to determine it own destiny. We have no wish to war with the Soviet Union – for we are a peaceful people who desire to live in peace with all other peoples."

"But it is difficult to settle or even discuss these problems in an atmosphere of intimidation. That is why this latest Soviet threat—or any other threat, which is made independently or in response to our actions this week--must and will be met with determination. Any hostile move anywhere in the world against the safety and freedom of peoples to whom we are committed--including in particular the brave people of West Berlin--will be met by whatever action is needed."

Not since the American Civil War (1861-1865) have we had so much to lose (economically, politically, financially, and spiritually) and so little to gain. Although the cry in the land is change, if we are not careful, we may end up trading more of our freedoms for these promised changes.

Our forefathers said it best when they wrote the following preliminary introduction to our Constitution. Let it always remind us of our heritage, our inheritance, and our future.

Preamble to the Constitution

We the People of the United States, in Order to form a more perfect Union, establish Justice, insure domestic Tranquility, provide for the common defence, promote the general Welfare, and secure the Blessings of Liberty to ourselves and our Posterity, do ordain and establish this Constitution for the United States of America.

(Chapter III)

They shall Ear his Ground, Reap his Harvest,
make his Instruments of War,
and Instruments of his Chariots

Winston Churchill said, "If you will not fight for your rights when you can easily win without bloodshed – if you will not fight when your victory will be sure and not too costly – then you may come to the moment when you will have to fight with all the odds against you and only a small chance of survival."

"There may even be a worse case: you may have to fight when there is no hope of victory, because it is better to perish than to live as slaves."

Today, as never before, we find ourselves as a nation and a

----

people in great straits. Unemployment is at an all time high (14.3 percent as of May 2015) (source: Moneycrashers), federal Pension Benefit Guaranty Corporation is $34 billion in debt (source: Washington Post), and Social Security's trustees forecast a current-dollar shortfall of $10 trillion. (source: Center on Budget and Policy Priorities)

The ten largest airlines are on the verge of bankruptcy (source: Chicago Times), and the number of Americans filing for bankruptcy in 2007 increased 40 percent over 2006. (source: Money.cnn)

Under pressure to meet combat needs, the Army and Marine Corps brought in significantly more recruits with felony convictions last year than in 2006, including some with manslaughter and sex crime convictions.

Data released by a congressional committee shows the number of soldiers admitted to the Army with felony records jumped from 249 in 2006 to 511 in 2007. And the number of Marines with felonies rose from 208 to 350.

Those numbers represent a fraction of the more than 180,000 recruits brought in by the active duty Army, Navy, Air Force and Marines during fiscal year ending Sept. 30, 2007. But they highlight a trend that has raised concerns both within the military and on Capitol Hill. (source: MSNBC)

David Segal, director of the Center for Research on Military Organization at the University of Maryland says, "There is no question that the force is stretched too thin. We have stopped treating the reserves as a force in reserve. Our volunteer army is closer to being broken today than ever before in its 30-year history."

If we possess the greatest array of weaponry ever produced in the history of the world (and we do), and we have the greatest armada of fighting ships and aircraft, and our fighting force is the best trained in the world, then why should it take us years to end a conflict?

And, even when we do win, without our continued presence, the country quickly sheds any changes made and ultimately returns to its old and evil ways (e.g., Vietnam, Somalia, and Kuwait).

The below list evidences the number of military deaths (battle related) since Jimmy Carter. (source: Joe Miller-Fact Checker)

Years	President	Total Combat Related Deaths
1977-1981	Jimmy Carter	4,772
1981-1989	Ronald Reagan	5,454
1989-1993	George Bush Sr.	4,508
1993-2000	Bill Clinton	13,417
2000-2008	George Bush Jr.	9,016

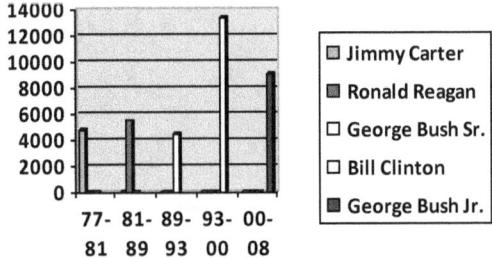

We've so integrated ourselves into the race to be the best that we've lost sight of how precious life is. In 2002 when then professional football player Pat Tillman resigned from the Arizona Cardinals and joined the Army Rangers, an elite group of fighters, the applauds and appreciative responses were endless.

Then 12 months later, the world was shocked to learn he died from what was later determined to be "friendly" fire. Sadly, his sacrifice has almost been forgotten.

When the Cold War ended, so ended the way we viewed the world as a place of danger and uncertainty. After Iraq invaded Kuwait and George Bush Sr. announced plans to halt the advance of Saddam Hussein, he declared a "New World Order."

While he was correct in saying that the world was about to change, it was not transformed in the manner he had envisioned. And although the reliance on multilateral institutions is still the norm for global governance today, the frosty clarity of that time has given way to a foggy bottom of differences, leaving us to search for solutions in order to remove the obstacles that abound for solving many of the world's problems. (source: A New World Order, Anne-Marie Slaughter, Joanne J. Myers)

The United States Department of Homeland Security (DHS) is a cabinet department of the United States federal government created in response to the September 11 attacks. Their primary responsibility is to protect the United States of America and U.S. Territories (including Protectorates) from terrorist attacks, man-made accidents, and natural disasters.

Whereas the Department of Defense is charged with military actions abroad, the Department of Homeland Security works in the civilian sphere to protect the United States within, at, and outside its borders. Its stated goal is to prepare for, prevent, and respond to domestic emergencies, particularly terrorism.

The Gulf War, 9-11, and other world developments have further necessitated the introduction of two dynamic legislative actions, Patriot Act (signed into law in 2001), and the Patriot Act II (revised the original Patriot Act in 2004).

The USA PATRIOT Act is an Act of Congress that was signed into law by President George W. Bush on October 26, 2001. Its title is a ten-letter backronym (USA PATRIOT) that stands for "Uniting and Strengthening America by Providing Appropriate Tools Required to Intercept and Obstruct Terrorism Act of 2001."

Patriot Act Articles

- Authority to intercept wire, oral, and electronic communications relating to terrorism,
- Authority to intercept wire, oral, and electronic communications relating to computer fraud and abuse offenses,
- Authority to share electronic, wire and oral interception information,
- Clarification of intelligence exceptions from limitations on interception and disclosure of wire, oral, and electronic communications.
- Roving surveillance authority under the Foreign

Intelligence Surveillance Act (FISA) of 1978

- Duration of FISA surveillance of non-United States persons who are agents of a foreign power,
- Seizure of voice-mail messages pursuant to warrants,
- Emergency disclosure of electronic communications to protect life and limb,
- Pen register and trap and trace authority under FISA, Access to records and other items under the FISA,
- Interception of computer trespasser communications, foreign intelligence information,
- Nationwide service of search warrants for electronic evidence,
- Civil liability for certain unauthorized disclosures,
- Immunity for compliance with FISA wiretap.

The USA PATRIOT Act II (Domestic Security Enhancement Act) expanded the powers of the United States federal government while simultaneously curtailing judicial review of these powers.
Provisions include:

- Removal of court-ordered prohibitions against police agencies spying on domestic groups.
- The Federal Bureau of Investigation would be granted powers to conduct searches and surveillance based on intelligence gathered in foreign countries without first obtaining a court order.
- Creation of a DNA database of suspected terrorists.

- Prohibition of any public disclosure of the names of alleged terrorists including those who have been arrested.

- Exemptions from civil liability for people and businesses who voluntarily turn private information over to the government. Criminalization of the use of encryption to conceal incriminating communications.

- Automatic denial of bail for persons accused of terrorism-related crimes, reversing the ordinary common law burden of proof principle. Persons charged with terrorists acts would be required to demonstrate why they should be released on bail rather than the government being required to demonstrate why they should be held.

- Expansion of the list of crimes eligible for the death penalty.

- The Environmental Protection Agency would be prevented from releasing "worst-case scenario" information to the public about chemical plants.

- United States citizens whom the government finds to be either members of, or providing material support to, terrorist groups could have their citizenship revoked and be deported to foreign countries.

Patriot Act II Articles

SECTION 501 (Expatriation of Terrorists) expands the Bush administration's "enemy combatant" definition to all American citizens who "may" have violated any provision of Section 802 of the first Patriot Act. Under Section 501 a US citizen engaging in lawful   activities can be grabbed off the street and thrown into a van never to be seen again.

SECTION 201 of the second Patriot Act makes it a criminal act for any member of the government or any citizen to release any information concerning the incarceration or whereabouts of detainees. It also states that law enforcement does not even have to tell the press who they have arrested and they never have to release the names.

SECTION 301 and **306** (Terrorist Identification Database) set up a national database of "suspected terrorists" and radically expands the database to   include   anyone   associated with suspected terrorist groups and anyone involved in crimes or having supported any group designated as "terrorist." These sections also set up a national DNA database for anyone on probation, or who has been on probation for any crime, and orders State governments to collect the DNA for the Federal government.

SECTION 312 gives immunity to law enforcement engaging in spying operations against the American people and would place substantial restrictions on court injunctions against Federal violations of civil rights across the board.

SECTION 103 allows the Federal government to use wartime martial law powers domestically and internationally without Congress declaring that a state of war exists.

SECTION 126 grants the government the right to mine the entire spectrum of public and private sector information from bank records to educational and medical records. This is the enacting law to allow ECHELON and the Total Information Awareness Network to break down any and all walls of privacy. The government states that they must look at everything to "determine" if individuals or groups might have a connection to terrorist groups. As you can now see, you are guilty until proven innocent.

SECTION 322 removes Congress from the extradition process and allows officers of the Homeland Security complex to extradite American citizens anywhere they wish. It also allows Homeland Security to secretly take individuals out of foreign countries.

King Solomon when dedicating the temple of the Lord prayed a prayer for himself and the nation (recorded in the sixth chapter of Second Chronicles).

"When the heaven is shut up, and there is no rain, because they have sinned against thee; yet if they pray toward this place, and confess thy name, and turn from their sin, when thou dost afflict them; Then hear thou from heaven, and forgive the sin of thy servants ... We have sinned, we have done amiss, and have dealt wickedly ... hear thou from the heavens, even from thy dwelling place, their prayer and their supplications, and maintain their cause, and forgive thy people which have sinned against thee" (II Chron. 6:26, 27, 37, 39).

In response, the Lord answered his prayer in the seventh chapter

----

with a powerful declaration,

"And the Lord appeared to Solomon by night, and said unto him, I have heard thy prayer, and have chosen this place to myself for an house of sacrifice" (II Chron. 7:12).

With all the confusion, uncertainty and paranoia in our world, I can only hope our president would pray a similar prayer of repentance.

His efforts, although unpopular, could change, delay or even stop the course we're now traveling – however, we must hurry, the hour draws near.

"He that hath an ear, let him hear what the Spirit saith unto the churches; To him that overcometh will I give to eat of the tree of life, which is in the midst of the paradise of God" (Rev. 2:7).

(Chapter IV)

Your Daughters shall be Confectionaries, Cooks, and Bakers

Today, women make up 48 percent of the nations work force (source: Human Resources). The quote, "Behind every successful man is a great woman," is starting to lose much of its luster as more and more women are establishing themselves as history making leaders.

Lucy Peng (CEO, Small & Micro Financial Services Group, Alibaba), Condoleezza Rice, Sheryl Sandberg (COO Facebook) Sheila C. Johnson, Maya Ying Lin, Rosalyn Sussman Yalow, Carly Fiorina, Andrea Jung, Anne Mulcahy, Meg Whitman, Adena Friedman (CO-President Nasdaq), and Marissa Meyer (CEO Yahoo) are only a few of the thousands of successful and influential women making headlines.

Yet, as the role of women changes, along with an increase in the number of working dads and moms, you can't help but wonder how these changes will affect the traditional family structure? A recent article titled, "Breakdown of the Family Structure," (Patrick Fagan) has some interesting points,

- By 1990, parents were on average, available 10 hours less per week to their children than they were in 1980 and 40 percent less than they were in 1965.

- In a Massachusetts Mutual poll, 33 percent of parents said they did not spend enough time with their preschool children and 46 percent said they did not spend enough time with their teenagers.

- A 1990 Los Angeles Times poll found that 57 percent of all fathers and 55 percent of all mothers felt guilty about spending too little time with their children. The poll also found that 73 percent of all married couples would have one parent stay home full-time with the children "if money were not an issue."

- A 1990 Yankelovich poll found that 57 percent of mothers would give up work indefinitely if they no longer needed the money.

- Reflecting the concern about mothers' absence, a 1998 poll by Wirthlin Worldwide found that 86 percent of mothers believe their children would do better if cared for by their mothers rather

----

than by day care providers.

Similarly, an increasing number of parents think too many children are being raised in childcare.

As the winds of change blow across the nation, and yes, change is coming; we see a subtle yet determined push to uproot the social, material and spiritual values inherent in our society.

And, if this trend continues, in ten years, this generation and all future generation will have irreversible scars as more women lessen their roles to shape [confectionaries], develop [cooks], and mold [bakers] the hearts and minds of our leaders of tomorrow.

Although roughly 20 percent of preschoolers in married households are cared for by their fathers ("stay home"), (source: Women's News, 6 June 2008), this shift has little affected the typical family structure. The consensus among many wives surveyed is that their husbands' de facto status (head of home) was never in question.

In fact, many wives are ecstatic with their husbands' new role. Sure, they have their day-to-day responsibilities, (childcare, cleaning, cooking, and laundry duties), but an added benefit is the greater stability this arrangement brings to their marriage and the raising of their children.

Stephanie from Connecticut says, "I haven't read much about this topic, but we are one of those rare households where my husband stays home full-time with our two children while I work. Although it suits us well, it's not been without its challenges."

"He and I know its best in the long run, but if he had his choice,

I would stay home and he would work. But life doesn't always happen as we would like, and we consider ourselves lucky that I have a position allowing him to stay home and maintain our comfortable lifestyle."

"We know the situation is temporary, until the kids are in school, so this helps on those days he feels like a constant diaper-changing and cleaning machine."

According to Professor Rolf Loeber of the University of Pittsburgh School of Medicine, "There is increasing evidence for an important critical period that occurs early in children's lives. At that time, youngsters' attachment to adult caretakers is formed. This helps them to learn pro-social skills and to unlearn any aggressive or acting out behaviors."

"The early experience of intense maternal affection is the basis for the development of a conscience and moral empathy with others."

"If a child's emotional attachment to his mother is disrupted during the first few years, permanent harm can be done to his capacity for emotional attachment to others. He will be less able to trust others and throughout his life will stay more distant emotionally from others.

Having many different caretakers during the first few years can lead to a loss of this sense of attachment for life and to antisocial behavior."

"Separation from the mother, especially between six months and three years of age, can lead to long lasting negative effects on behavior and emotional development.

Severe maternal deprivation is a critical ingredient of juvenile delinquency: As John Bowlby, the father of attachment research, puts it, "Theft, like rheumatic fever, is a disease of childhood, and, as in rheumatic fever, attacks in later life are frequently in the nature of recurrences."

A child's emotional attachment to his mother is powerful in other ways. For example, even after a period of juvenile delinquency, a young man's ability to become emotionally attached to his wife can make it possible for him to turn away from crime.

This capacity is rooted in the very early attachment to his mother. We also know that a weak marital attachment resulting in separation or divorce accompanies a continuing life of crime.

Many family conditions can weaken a mother's attachment to her young child. Perhaps the mother herself is an emotionally unattached person. The mother could be so lacking in family and emotional support that she cannot fill the emotional needs of the child. She could return to work, or be forced to return to work, too soon after the birth of her child.

Or, while she is at work, there could be a change in the personnel responsible for the child's day care. The more prevalent these conditions, the less likely a child will be securely attached to his mother and the more likely he will be hostile and aggressive.

The mother's relationship with her children during this early period is also relevant to the debate over childcare. According to Professor James Q. Wilson of the University of California at Los Angeles, the extended absence of a working mother from her child during the early critical stages of the child's emotional development increases the risk of delinquency.

Specifically, says Stephen Cernkovich and Peggy Giordano, "Maternal employment affects behavior indirectly, through such factors as lack of supervision, loss of direct control, and attenuation of close relationships."

"Thus, forcing a young single mother to return to work too soon after the birth of her baby is bad public policy. Unfortunately, the Clinton Administration's welfare reform bill would do just that." (Patrick F. Fagan)

In today's typical two-parent (dad and mom), 2.5 kid home, you'll find, 2-3 cars, 3-4 televisions, three portable entertainment systems (i.e., Wii, PS2, Xbox, Nintendo), four cellular phones, two iPhones, and of course your standard Internet access.

The average 8-10 year old spends between 4-6 hours each day playing one or a combination of these systems. Sadly, in many instances these devices are now raising our children.

Martin Luther said, *Therefore, it is of the greatest importance for every married man to pay closer, more thorough, and continuous attention to the health of his child's soul than to the body which he has begotten, and to regard his child as nothing else but an eternal treasure God has commanded him to protect, and so prevent the World, the flesh, and the Devil from stealing the child away and*

----

bringing him to destruction. "

As society screams for change, we're witnessing a complete transformation in our decision making: in the family, the political scene, and even in the church. We're becoming a people that walk by sight, intellect and popular opinion.

The result is a generation oblivious to the inherent dangers of a complacent and socially acceptable existence. Sadly, the "Live for today" spirit has garnered so great a following, that it now shapes our concept of right and wrong.

In 1991, Congress voted to repeal the law excluding women from serving in combat areas, and combat vessels. Women today not only make up some 15 percent of the United States active duty forces, but 11 percent of the soldiers in Iraq and Afghanistan.

Shockingly, nearly a third of all female veterans report an instance of sexual assault or rape while in the military. And another 71 to 90 percent say they were sexually harassed by the men with whom they served.

This sort of abuse drastically increases the risk and intensity of Post-Traumatic Stress Disorder (P.T.S.D.). One study found that female soldiers who were sexually assaulted were nine times more likely to show symptoms of this disorder than those who weren't.

Sexual harassment by itself is so destructive, another study revealed, it causes the same rates of post-traumatic stress in women as combat does in men. And, rape can lead to other medical crises, including diabetes, asthma, chronic pelvic pain, eating disorders,

----

miscarriages and hypertension.

The threat of post-traumatic stress has risen in recent years as women's roles in war have changed. More of them now come under fire, suffer battle wounds and kill the enemy, just as men do. As women return for repeat tours, usually redeploying with their same units, many must go back to war with the same man (or men) who abused them.

This leaves these women as threatened by their own comrades as by the war itself. Yet the combination of sexual assault and combat has barely been acknowledged or studied. (source: Helen Benedict, NY Times)

The 2000 Veterans Administration (VA) study reports that 55 percent of women experienced sexual harassment in the military. And, a 2005 study estimates that more than half of women in the reserves and National Guard suffered sexual assault or harassment during their service, according to news reports. (source: NPR and AP)

Continuing a 12-year decline, the U.S. birth rate has dropped to the lowest level since national data have been available, according to statistics just released by the Centers for Disease Control (CDC). The rate of births among teenagers also fell to a new record low, continuing a decline that began in 1991.

The birth rate fell to 13.9 per 1,000 persons in 2002, down from 14.1 per 1,000 in 2001 and down a full 17 percent from the recent peak in 1990 (16.7 per 1,000), according to a new CDC report, "Births: Preliminary Data for 2002." CDC analysts say the birth rate is dropping as the increasing life span of Americans results in a smaller proportion of women of child childbearing age.

The birth rate in the U.S. for the first time in 35 years has declined to an almost alarming proportion, 2:1. This means for every two deaths there is only one birth (source: Washington Post).

If this same pattern continues for another 50 years, the population of the U.S. could shrink from its current 300 million, to less than 200 million.

In 1920, women won the right to vote. In 1923, Senator Curtis and Representative Anthony (nephew of suffragist Susan B. Anthony), both Republicans introduced the Equal Rights Amendment (ERA) in Congress. Alice Paul, head of the National Women's Party, who led the suffrage campaign, authored this amendment.

Since women first gathered and marched in opposition to laws of inequality, little could they envision the strides and advancements of the next 70 years.

1923: Alice Paul and the National Woman's Party succeed in having a constitutional amendment proposing equal rights for women introduced in Congress. This amendment was revised in 1943 to become the Equal Rights Amendment.

1929: Genevieve Cline is the first woman appointed to serve as a federal judge.

1945: Eleanor Roosevelt becomes the first former first lady to be appointed to a public position when she assumes the post of U.N. delegate.

1961: "The President's Commission on the Status of Women," is created by President John F. Kennedy, and is chaired by Eleanor Roosevelt until her death in 1962. The group examined labor laws, income, education and legal representation for women.

1963: The Equal Pay Act establishes equal pay for men and women performing the same job duties.

1964: Title VII of the Civil Rights Act bars employment discrimination by private employers, employment agencies and unions based on race, sex and other grounds.

1966: The National Organization for Women (NOW) is formed to function as a civil rights organization for women. Betty Friedan is a founder and the first president.

1970: The Equal Rights Amendment is reintroduced into Congress.

1971: Ms. Magazine, edited by Gloria Steinem, first appears as an insert in New York magazine.

1972: Title IX of the Education Amendment requires equal opportunity to an education.

1972: Congress passes the Equal Employment Opportunity Act, giving the EEOC power to take legal action to enforce its rulings.

1981: Sandra Day O'Connor is the first woman appointed to the U.S. Supreme Court.

1982: The Equal Rights Amendment fails to achieve ratification.

1984: Geraldine Ferraro is the first woman vice-presidential

----

candidate of a major political party.

1998: Eileen Collins, who was the first female shuttle pilot in 1995, becomes the first woman to command a space shuttle mission.

Our prisons are bulging with kids that society has failed. Instead of focusing on building our corner or niche in the world, we need to evaluate and prioritize our future, a future that includes the success of our children.

Vandell Savage a villain in the "Here After" episode of the Justice League cartoon series, made a simple yet profound statement regarding his obsession to take over the world. "It took me 30,000 years to figure out that my lust for power and control was meaningless."

If we're to see an awakening in our generation, four things must happen,

- A realization of our wayward ways,
- A willingness to turn from these ways,
- A trust in the righteousness and salvation of a Thrice Holy God,
- An abrogation [denial] of self and a commitment to follow the Lord.

Admittedly, this is not easy or popular. Yet, if we are to turn the tide of darkness hovering over the land, we must act now –

". . . the night cometh when no man can work" (Jn. 9:4).

"To every thing there is a season, and a time to every purpose under the heaven: A time to be born, and a time to die; a time to plant, and a time to pluck up that which is planted; A time to kill, and a time to heal; a time to break down, and a time to build up; A time to weep, and a time to laugh; a time to mourn, and a time to dance"

"A time to cast away stones, and a time to gather stones together; a time to embrace, and a time to refrain from embracing; A time to get, and a time to lose; a time to keep, and a time to cast away; A time to rend, and a time to sew; a time to keep silence, and a time to speak; A time to love, and a time to hate; a time of war, and a time of peace" (Ecc. 3:1-8).

(Chapter V)

He will Take your Fields,
your Vineyards, your Olive Yards,
and give them to his Servants

"This is not a field of specialty for me, but my general feeling is that the recession will be longer and deeper than most people think. This will not be short and shallow. I think consumers are feeling gas and food prices, and not feeling they've got a lot of money for other things." —**Warren Buffet**

"There seems to be a lot of agreement out there that the economy is falling. People certainly seem nervous. Consumer confidence is at its lowest level since we went into the Iraq war. Lots of concerns out there. And you can't blame Americans. You've seen what's going on in the housing market. That is folks' biggest asset" —**Gerri Willis**

As we approach the midpoint of 2008, our economic picture has a bleak outlook, and that's putting it mildly.

It seems the only constant in our high paced society is the unknown. While the Democrats and Republicans point fingers at each other, we [the American people] are somewhere in the middle, caught in the throes of their innuendos, and accusatory statements.

According to research analyst, The Barna Group, the proportion of households that tithe income to their church - that is, give at least ten percent of their income to that ministry - dropped by 62% from 2001 to 2002. In 2001 8% tithed 10% of their income compared to just 3% during 2002.

The strength of the family unit is intertwined with the practice of religion. Churchgoers are more likely to be married, less likely to be divorced or single, and more likely to manifest high levels of satisfaction in marriage.

- Church attendance is the most important predictor of marital stability and happiness.

- The regular practice of religion is instrumental in helping poor persons move out of poverty.

- Regular church attendance helps young people in particular to escape the poverty of inner-city life.

- Religious beliefs and practices contribute substantially to the formation of personal moral criteria and sound moral judgment.

- Regular religious practice generally inoculates individuals against a host of social problems, including suicide, drug abuse, out-of-wedlock births, crime, and divorce.

- Regular religious practice has powerful mental health benefits, including lower rates of depression (a modern epidemic), more self-esteem, and greater family and marital happiness.

- Religious beliefs and practices are a major source of strength during recovery from alcoholism, drug addiction, and marital breakdown.

- Regular practice of religion is good for personal physical health. It is positively associated with longevity, recovery from illness, and lower incidence of serious diseases.

Professor Allan Bergin, a research psychologist who was honored by the American Psychological Association with its top award in 1990, said in accepting the award this,

"Some religious influences have a modest impact; whereas another portion seems like the mental equivalent of nuclear energy...The more powerful portion can provide transcendent conviction or commitment and is sometimes manifested in dramatic personal healing or transformation."

"YOU DO NOT have to have a temperament inclined to alarmism to recognize the multiple signs of decay around us in the United States today."

"The dollar is down. Financial markets have been shaken. Productivity is not good. The stock market cannot decide whether to remain in manic mode, or reverse itself into depressed. The one thing we can be sure of is that it is not really trustworthy, because the decay of regulatory authority and of business ethics in general has left it without reliable standards."

"We are mired in wars that have accomplished little or nothing of value, and prove that we are stretched too thin. Some of us are in a panic over illegal immigration into the US. Our medical system is abandoning a large portion of the populace."

"The country's infrastructure shows serious signs of decay, from unusable school buildings to fraying road systems, and to the occasional collapsing bridge. And we have still not made much headway on the rebuilding of New Orleans."

"We cannot expect commiseration from others, who may well have grown tired of living in our shadow for the past few generations. As this reality begins to sink in, it leads to a degree of introspection, as we reflect on how things could deteriorate so quickly."

"Traditionally, this is the opportunity for religious leaders to speak of judgment, and admonish the people for their sins. Unfortunately, it is not a helpful move, since the lists of sins put forward by right-wing and left-wing Christians are incommensurable. Is sexual laxness destroying us, or hostility to illegal immigrants? Is it the teaching of evolution in state schools, or indifference to the environment?"

"It is easier to argue on the side of the left. The present regime's subservience to the rich, its hostility to all kinds of regulation, and its quasi-messianic effort to impose democracy on

----

Iraq has all contributed directly to most of our current ills. But our religious traditions, with their roots in Puritanism, still find it more natural to place the blame on individual morals."

"In any case, religious leaders might better devote themselves not to listing faults and assigning blame, but to offering grounds for hope: hope that we can yet remedy some of our failings makes repentance possible. It creates the possibility of commitment and of a new sense of community."

"That may also be the most valuable thing the current competitors for the presidency could be offering." (source: Reverend/Dr. Bill Countryman)

At least 85 percent of all immigrants coming to the U.S. do so in hopes of finding a better life (source: Elizabeth Arizaga). Initially there is little interest in politics or what part was leading the country: this was America, land of the brave and home of the free – a place where they could start over.

We however are living in an America that has a different ethnicity than 50 years ago – a truer depiction of the inscription on the Statue of Liberty.

The New Colossus
(Emma Lazarus)

Not like the brazen giant of Greek fame,
With conquering limbs astride from land to land,
Here at our sea-washed, sunset gates shall stand,
A mighty woman with a torch, whose flame,

Is the imprisoned lightning, and her name,
Mother of exiles. From her beacon-hand,
Glows world-wide welcome; her mild eyes command,
The air-bridged harbor that twin cities frame.

"Keep, ancient lands, your storied pomp!" cries she,
With silent lips. "Give me your tired, your poor,
Your huddled masses yearning to breathe free,
The wretched refuse of your teeming shore,
Send these, the homeless, tempest-tost, to me,
I lift my lamp beside the golden door!"

Sadly, many of these immigrants weep openly as they see the same signs of capitalism rearing its ugly head in America that ravaged their country.

Nguyễn Văn Thiệu said, "I came from Vietnam to build a life for my family in America. I owned no property in Vietnam, and I paid the government almost 90 percent in taxes. We lived in a capitalist society where we had no rights. I now see the same signs of capitalism slowly raising their head all around me."

Capitalism is defined as an economic system based on private ownership of capital. The government in other words owns everything, and the people live in government houses and work in government factories (Naomi Klein, "The Shock Doctrine: The Rise of Disaster Capitalism").

The government came to own property in much the same way

---

they are stepping in to rescue businesses and homeowners today – by default. Could our society become capitalistic or even socialistic? Only time will tell.

The Guinness Book of World Records holds Edna Parker of Shelbyville, Indiana as the oldest person in the world. She was born on April 20, 1893 and is 115 years old. Edna has lived through 7 wars, 20 presidents, the electric light bulb, the depression, the first atomic bomb, desegregation, the first man on the moon, and Watergate.

Yet, she has never known a time of world peace: a time when greed was not the driving factor, and where the agape love of the Lord (unconditional love) prevailed over the entirety of the land. However, that time of world peace is soon to be realized in the not to distant future.

President Bush on several occasions has said he believes a peace settlement is possible between Israel and Palestine before the end of his tenure. I remind Mr. Bush that his predecessor, Mr. Bill Clinton also attempted this same feat without success.

The book of Daniel tells us that a peace agreement will be signed (Daniel 7:21), but brokered by one that is yet to come, a Syrian Jew (Daniel 10:40).

While we chant "change," "change," and await the results of the elections in November, let's note some of the rights and freedoms we've already lost – all without a fight.

Through the enactment of the USA PATRIOT Act and

subsequent executive directives and regulations, essential rights and freedoms that were once guaranteed to all individuals have been substantially degraded.

Many Americans still do not realize the significance of what we have lost. The resulting expansion of government powers and the erosion of 1st, 4th, 5th, 6th, 8th and 14th Amendment rights and freedoms have forever transformed the United States.

1st AMENDMENT FREEDOM OF SPEECH

• The Patriot Act broadly expands the official definition of terrorism, so that many domestic groups that engage in nonviolent civil disobedience could very well find themselves labeled as terrorists.

• The Government may now prosecute librarians or keepers of any other records if they reveal that the government requested information on their clients or members in the course of an investigation. It has become a crime for these individuals to try to safeguard your privacy or to tell you that you are under investigation.

1st AMENDMENT FREEDOM OF ASSOCIATION

• Government agents may now monitor the First Amendment protected activities of religious and political institutions, and then infiltrate these groups with no suspicion of criminal activity. This is a return to domestic spying on law-abiding religious and political groups.

• You may now be the subject of a government investigation simply because of the political, activist, or advocacy groups you are involved in, or the statements you make within these groups.

1st AMENDMENT RIGHT TO ACCESS GOVERNMENT INFORMATION

• A U.S. Department of Justice directive actively encourages federal, state, and local officials to resist and/or limit access to government records through Freedom of Information Act (FOIA) requests.

• The Government has conducted immigration hearings in secret behind closed doors. Such proceedings were once open to the public. Hundreds, if not thousands, of immigrants have already been deported in secret.

4th AMENDMENT FREEDOM FROM UNREASONABLE SEARCHES and SEIZURES

• Law Enforcement authorities may now conduct secret searches and wiretaps in your home or office without showing "probable cause." They need only to claim that intelligence gathering is "a significant purpose" of their intrusion, even when the primary goal is ordinary law enforcement. They may also monitor where and to whom you send and receive e-mail, or where you go on the Internet, recording every e-mail address and website you have been in contact with.

• Law Enforcement may now demand any personal records held

----

by any source including your doctor, employer, accountant, or library. All they have to do is claim that it is related to an investigation into "terrorism." The record keepers may not reveal that your records were provided to the government.

• Judicial oversight of secret searches has been effectively minimized. The Patriot Act directs judges to consent to secret searches based only on the Government's assertion that a "significant" purpose of an investigation is gathering information related to "terrorism," as the government defines it.

5th AMENDMENT RIGHT TO DUE PROCESS and FREEDOM FROM BEING HELD WITHOUT CHARGE

• Americans can now be jailed without a formal charge and without the right to confront the witnesses or evidence against them. American citizens are now being held in military jails without charge and without a clear path of appeal for their indefinite confinement.

• Hundreds of Arab, Muslim and South Asian men were rounded up in the Ashcroft raids following September 11, and held for weeks without charges until all were cleared of terrorism charges.

6th AMENDMENT RIGHT TO LEGAL REPRESENTATION

• Hundreds of U.S. residents have been detained for months at a time, and denied access to the advice and advocacy of an attorney. The Government may now monitor conversations between attorneys

----

and clients in federal jails.

• The Bush Administration filed papers in court arguing that an American citizen held in a military jail without charge should be denied access to legal counsel because such access would interfere with the process of his interrogation.

6th AMENDMENT RIGHT TO A SPEEDY AND PUBLIC TRIAL

• The U.S. Government may now jail its residents and citizens indefinitely without charge and without a public trial.

8th AMENDMENT FREEDOM FROM CRUEL AND UNUSUAL PUNISHMENTS

• The U.S. Government has taken into custody individuals they identify as "material witnesses," transported them across the country, and held them for months in solitary confinement without charge or contact with their family.

• According to the Justice Department's own Inspector General, immigrant men rounded up in the Ashcroft raids following September 11 and held in the Metropolitan Detention Center in Brooklyn, NY were subjected to a pattern of "physical and verbal abuse."

14th AMENDMENT RIGHT TO EQUAL PROTECTION

• Over 82,000 men from Arab, Muslim and South Asian countries registered with the Government under the Special Registration program. Over 13,000 are now in deportation

----

proceedings. None have been charged with terrorism.

Although the infringement of these rights may seem insignificant, realize this, what's lost will not be returned – at least not without a fight! And, if those rights and freedoms can be so easily lost, others are not far behind.

While it's true that a bill passed in Iowa limiting the amount of acreage farmed each year does not directly affect the price of a potato crop in Idaho, we need to understand that we're in this together: your hurt should be my hurt, and your pain my pain. If we fail to understand this simple principle, our independent thinking will eventually be the end of us.

Get involved. Write your congressional representative, and senator. Send an email to the Democratic and Republican camps voicing your opinions and objections. They represent your voice in Congress and the political arena. These specialty groups do listen. Yet they can only act on the concerns you voice to them.

Democratic Party – www.my.democrats.org/page/s/contact-the-democrats

Republican Party – email: ecampaign@gop.com

Contact Congress Today!
The Capitol switchboard number is (202) 224-3121

To contact your Senators,
www.senate.gov/general/contact_information/senators_cfm.cfm

To contact your House Representatives,

www.house.gov/representatives/find/

To contact the White House

www.whitehouse.gov/contact/

Vote Monitor: Monitor your elected official's voting record to make sure he/she is reflecting YOUR voice in Washington.

Sign up at: www.congress.org/congressorg/megavote/

Take Action on Issues

www.nea.org/home/19546.htm

If you don't say anything, your lands [rights], your crops [freedoms] and your vineyards [privileges] will all be lost.

(Chapter VI)

He will take the Tenth of your Seed,
Sheep and Vineyards,
and give to his Officers,
and to his Servants

Although the chronicles of our human history are filled with page after page of cruel and barbaric behavior; we have also proven to be a people of great mercy, compassion and tenderness.

Why such schizophrenic behavior? Sadly, our nature since sins inception (Genesis 3:4-7) is bent toward darkness.

Maurice Henry Hewlett said, *"Man is a creature of social instinct condemned by his nature to be solitary. Creatures in all*

*outward respects similar to himself are awhirl about him. They
cannot help him, nor he them; he cannot even be sure, for all he may
assume it, that they share his hope and calling."*

Our emotional reactions come about as our receptors of feeling
are stimulated by things we touch, taste, smell or hear. Other
external acts or actions stimulate our logical or intellectual reactions.
Thus, life is divided between two distinct camps, the body and the
mind. Admittedly, there are events that identifiably cause us a
greater emotional and physical reaction than others do. (source: Mark
Pettinelli)

In election years emotions, expectations and disappointments all
have a tendency to run the gauntlet from the high to the low. "What
new ideas will come forth?" "Will society change for the better or
the worst?" "How will this election affect me personally, socially
and financially?" "What will our society look like after the next four
years?"

In December 2007, Senator Barack Obama and several of his
constituents introduced a bill to the 110th Congress titled "The
Global Poverty Act." This bill requires the President to develop and
implement a comprehensive strategy to further the United States
foreign policy objective.

We are to do this by, √promoting the reduction of global
poverty, √the elimination of extreme global poverty, and √the
achievement of the Millennium Development Goal (aim is to reduce
by one-half the proportion of people worldwide, between 1990 and
2015 that live on less than $1 per day).

On March 22, 2002, President George W. Bush stated, "We fight against poverty because hope is an answer to terror. We fight against poverty because opportunity is a fundamental right to human dignity. We fight against poverty because faith requires it and conscience demands it. We fight against poverty with a growing conviction that major progress is within our reach."

On the surface, the bill seems harmless, yet under closer scrutiny, the bill reveals how the U.S. has methodically evolved into a global partner. We no longer lead the world but share [collaborate] with countries economically, politically, financially, and militarily for the good of the people. The following stratagems are listed in the bill for its implementation:

(1) Continued investment or involvement in existing United States initiatives related to international poverty reduction such as: the United States Leadership Against HIV/AIDS, Tuberculosis, and Malaria Act of 2003 (22 U.S.C. 7601 et seq.), the Millennium Challenge Act of 2003 (22 U.S.C. 7701 et seq.), and trade preference programs for developing countries, such as the African Growth and Opportunity Act (19 U.S.C. 3701 et seq.).

(2) Leveraging United States trade policy where possible to enhance economic development prospects for developing countries.

(3) Coordinating efforts and working in cooperation with developed and developing countries, international organizations, and international financial institutions.

(4) Mobilizing and leveraging the participation of businesses,

----

United States and international nongovernmental organizations, civil society, and public-private partnerships.

(5) Coordinating the goal of poverty reduction with other development goals, such as combating the spread of preventable diseases such as HIV/AIDS, tuberculosis, and malaria, increasing access to potable water and basic sanitation, reducing hunger and malnutrition, and improving access to and quality of education at all levels regardless of gender.

(6) Integrating principles of sustainable development and entrepreneurship into policies and programs.

Jesus told His disciples, *"For ye have the poor always with you; but me ye have not always"* (Matt. 26:11). This is a stern warning regarding our priorities. While taking care of the poor is important and necessary, simply meeting their day-to-day needs is temporal at best.

A disproportional allocation of resources exists in the world and continues since Adam's fall in the garden. Unfortunately, this inequity will not change or right itself through new leadership, new ideas or new laws, for no edict can legislate out the depravity and darkness of the human heart.

In our fast-paced society, it's almost impossible to find an untainted depiction of the innocence of life. The birth of a baby comes close but even that is scarred by the fallen nature of Adam. Sadly, we are so busy running from one "fire" to another fire that we overlook what truly is important and eternal – life itself.

As news agencies continue reporting on the woes of our economy, a feeling of panic and fear is slowly settling over the land. In response to these concerns, consumers [all of us] are buying less, investing less and traveling less. The results of our actions equal a recession.

A recession is a significant decline in economic activity spread across the economy, lasting more than a few months, normally visible in real Gross Domestic Products (GDP): real income, employment, industrial production, and wholesale-retail sales.

A recession begins just after the economy reaches a peak of activity and ends as the economy reaches its trough. Between trough and peak, the economy is in an expansion. Expansion is the normal state of the economy; most recessions are brief and they have been rare in recent decades.

Are we in a recession? Unemployment is one of the most telling signs that things aren't doing so great. In case you're wondering, the unemployment rate just hit 5% at the end of last year, marking a new two-year high.

Most everyone dreams of owning a home someday, so when such a popular market takes a massive hit; it can trickle down throughout the entire economy. And, if you've picked up a newspaper or magazine anytime within the past several months, you should be well aware that the housing market has seen much better days to say the least.

When financial times are tough, there are less jobs being

created, in addition to possible layoffs at current companies.

When the price of gas has you seriously considering folding your massive, manly frame into a dainty little hybrid car, it's another sign that a recession may be coming. High gas prices mean less driving, and less driving means less spending. A cycle could easily spiral out of control if the numbers on those price boards keep climbing.

More than half the 16 states reporting deficits this year have cut spending, including $1 billion by Florida lawmakers last year and across-the-board cuts in Nevada. At least eight states are debating raising taxes or fees, including a proposed $1-per-pack cigarette tax increase in Massachusetts to raise $175 million.

Twelve states, including Georgia, Idaho and Illinois, reported that personal income tax collection was failing to meet estimates, and in eight of these, collections were even below a reduced forecast.

Many states, including Alabama, Arizona, Massachusetts, Minnesota, Nevada and Wisconsin, plan to tap their rainy day funds, which contain money set aside for fiscal emergencies. Nevada may use its entire rainy day balance.

The finances of many states have deteriorated so badly that they appear to be in a recession, regardless of whether that's true for the nation as a whole, a survey of all 50 state fiscal directors concludes.

The situation is grim in Delaware, with a $69 million gap this year and bleak in California, with a projected $16 billion budget

----

shortfall over the next two years, the report said. Florida does not expect a rapid turnaround in revenue   because   of the prolonged real estate slump there.

Yet, with so much in this world in a chaotic state, we continue to ignore the obvious and cry "change."

During the debates over the North American Free Trade Agreement (NAFTA) and the World Trade Organization (WTO), U.S. farmers were made grand promises by the agreements' supporters.

They were told that by opening overseas markets, the pacts would cure the U.S. farm economy's woes, and that farmers would export their way to wealth.

With each new trade agreement since, farmers have been promised that they are just one trade agreement away from riches thanks to trade. Many farmers believed the promises and supported NAFTA and WTO and then later pushed for the grant of Permanent Normal Trade Relations with China to facilitate the Asian country's entry into the WTO.

The reality however has been the opposite: not only did U.S. agricultural producers not gain, but many also suffered serious damage. Trade flows did increase, but food imports into the United States outpaced U.S. exports. Unimaginably, in 2005, the United States became   a   net food importer – with an unprecedented food trade deficit of nearly $370 million.

The WTO required all signatory nations to eliminate quotas and other supply management programs. Through a process called "tariff-ication," quotas were translated into tariffs and then reduced over phase-in periods. The WTO also required signatory nations to eliminate various support programs.

The vehicle for many of these changes was the 1996 "Freedom to Farm Act," which eliminated various supply management and support programs designed to safeguard farmers against weather and market fluctuations that had been in place since the New Deal. As nations worldwide eliminated supply management, global production jumped, markets were glutted and commodity prices plummeted.

While the grain trading and food processing firms who helped write the WTO agricultural rules and the 1996 Farm Bill made record profits, U.S. farm income declined.

Many farms in fact went bankrupt. Meanwhile, Congress' ability to return to supply management and other proven-to-work programs was foreclosed by U.S. WTO obligations.

During the NAFTA-WTO period, nearly 300,000 family farmers have gone under, and the price paid for inputs has outstripped the price received by farmers for their products. During the NAFTA-WTO era, net farm income (minus government payments) declined 13 percent for family farmers.

As the trade agreements massively increased imports of the same commodities produced by U.S. farmers, prices declined. Even when U.S. production and export volumes increased, farm income declined. (source: Public Citizen's Global Trade Watch)

I propose we swallow our pride, lay aside our unbelief and look objectively, yet reverently to the Word of God. It alone encapsulates our past, defines our present and foretells our future. The choice and decisions are ours to make.

"But it shall come to pass, if thou wilt not hearken unto the voice of the Lord thy God, to observe to do all his commandments and his statutes which I command thee this day; that all these curses shall come upon thee, and overtake thee: Cursed shalt thou be in the city, and cursed shalt thou be in the field. Cursed shall be thy basket and thy store. Cursed shall be the fruit of thy body, and the fruit of thy land, the increase of thy kine, and the flocks of thy sheep."

"Cursed shalt thou be when thou comest in, and cursed shalt thou be when thou goest out. The Lord shall send upon thee cursing, vexation, and rebuke, in all that thou settest thine hand unto for to do, until thou be destroyed, and until thou perish quickly; because of the wickedness of thy doings, whereby thou hast forsaken me" (Deut. 28:15-20).

(Chapter VII)

He will take your Menservants,
Maidservants, your young Men,
and your Asses, to his Work

Under the Fair Labor Standards Act of 1938, minimum wage was set at $.25 per hour. This was the governments attempt to establish minimum living standards for workers engaged directly or indirectly in interstate commerce, including those involved in production of goods bound for such commerce.

Over the next 70 years, minimum wage has risen and fallen 26 times. Today [2015] it stands at $7.25 per hour. The weekly salary for those working 40 hours a week at minimum wage is $290.00 before taxes (Federal, State and FICA).

Although this salary would be more than sufficient for the basic amenities of life (e.g., car, home, utilities, insurance, and food) in most third world countries, in the U.S., families are working 2.5 jobs at minimum wage to pay for these necessities.

According to a report from the Department of Health and Human Services, "The Comprehensive Child Development Program (C.C.D.P.) was an innovative attempt by the Administration on Children, Youth, and Families (A.C.Y.F.) to ensure the delivery of early and comprehensive services with the aim of enhancing child development and helping low-income families achieve economic self-sufficiency.

C.C.D.P. grantees included universities, hospitals, public and private nonprofit organizations, and school districts. The total cost of C.C.D.P. averaged $15,768 per family per year (excluding the research costs), or about $47,000 for each family over the five years of operation. Each local C.C.D.P. grantee was to,

- intervene as early as possible in children's lives,
- involve the entire family,
- ensure the delivery of comprehensive social services to address the intellectual, social emotional, and physical needs of infants and young children in the household;
- ensure the delivery of services to enhance parents' ability to contribute to the overall development of their children and achieve economic and social self-sufficiency; and
- ensure continuous services until children enter elementary

----

school at the kindergarten or first grade level....

"Across the 21 projects, 4,410 families were included in the evaluation—2,213 families were assigned to C.C.D.P. and another 2,197 families were assigned to the control group (no special services given to them).... Exactly the same changes observed in C.C.D.P. families occurred in control group families...."

"Five years after the program began; C.C.D.P. had no statistically significant impacts on the economic self-sufficiency of participating mothers, or on their parenting skills. Mothers in the control group performed as well on these measures as C.C.D.P. mothers....C.C.D.P. had no meaningful impacts on the cognitive or social-emotional development of participating children. Children in the control group performed as well on these measures as children in C.C.D.P. Nor did C.C.D.P. have any impacts on children's health or on birth outcomes for children born subsequent to the focus children...."

"The length of time that a family was enrolled in C.C.D.P. was sometimes associated with a statistically significant difference in the outcomes achieved by that family, but those differences were not educationally or substantively meaningful." (source: The Breakdown of the Family-Patrick F. Fagan)

Social Security in the United States is a social insurance program funded through dedicated payroll taxes called Federal Insurance Contributions Act (FICA).

Tax deposits are formally entrusted to Federal Old-Age and

Survivors Insurance Trust Fund, or Federal Disability Insurance Trust Fund, Federal Hospital Insurance Trust Fund or the Federal Supplementary Medical Insurance Trust Fund. The main part of the program is sometimes abbreviated O.A.S.D.I. (Old Age, Survivors, and Disability Insurance) or R.S.D.I. (Retirement, Survivors, and Disability Insurance).

When initially signed into law by President Franklin Roosevelt in 1935, the term Social Security covered unemployment insurance as well. The term, in everyday speech, is used only to refer to the benefits for retirement, disability, survivorship, and death, which are the four main benefits provided by traditional private-sector pension plans.

In 2004, the U.S. Social Security system paid out almost $500 billion in benefits. By dollars paid, the U.S. Social Security program is the largest government program in the world and the single greatest expense in the federal budget, with 20.9% for social security and 20.4% for Medicare.

There are several problems with Social Security. (That is, besides the fact that there is no Constitutional authority for the Federal Government to set up a universal retirement system for its citizenry.)

First, the system is unsustainable over the long term.

Social Security helped to increase unemployment during the Great Depression.

The rate of return is lower than what could be obtained with

----

private investments.

Even though it's really a welfare program disguised as a retirement program, there's no means testing. (source: Donald A. Tevault)

In the eighties and nineties, entrepreneurs were springing up all over the land, yet the number of entrepreneurs fell by 25 percent worldwide this year, mirroring a general decline in economic growth, according to a new study of 37 countries.

Why the drop off? The reasons are varied, but there seems to be a feeling that our society has changed, and new and different ideas and ways are not as easily accepted as in previous years.

Some have even gone so far as to say that a conspiracy exists within the government to socialize our weakened economy. Whatever the reason, the spirit of entrepreneurship has almost died – and with it a spirit of growth, expansion and leadership.

Italy and France saw 42 and 57 percent declines, respectively, in the number of entrepreneurs, and Japan's rate dropped 65 percent, from 5.19 percent of the labor force to 1.81.

The U.S. decline was not statistically significant -- from 11.1 percent last year to 10.5 percent this year -- but its rate fell sharply the prior year, according to the study.

"Entrepreneurial activity is related to growth in GDP," said Larry W. Cox, an author of the study and director of research at the Ewing Marion Kauffman Foundation, which funded the study."

"If your economy is doing well, you're going to have a higher level of entrepreneurial activity, all else being equal," Cox said,

---

adding that the U.S.'s rate might have leveled in response to signs that the economy is stabilizing."

"There are about 460 million entrepreneurs worldwide, and Thailand tops the chart with 19 percent of its labor force actively entrepreneurial. Japan has the lowest rate, at 2 percent, according to the study."

"Japan has not only a culture favoring risk-taking and individualism but also an infrastructure that offers start-up funding, which puts the U.S. at a higher rate than most developed countries, said Andrew Zacharakis, professor of entrepreneurship at Babson College."

"About 6 percent of our adult population has invested in a new company (not stocks) within the last three years," Zacharakis said. "That adds another $100 billion on top of venture capital sources for equity ... The fuel is there to drive this entrepreneurial engine." (source: Andrea Coombes, CBS Market Watch)

The greatest concentration of millionaires per capita is within the U.S., and three of the top ten richest people in the world are from the U.S. However, within the U.S. roughly 12% to 15% of the people live below the federal poverty line at any given point in time, and roughly 40% falling below the poverty line at some time within a 10-year time span.

While there remains some controversy of whether or not the official poverty threshold over or understates poverty, the United States has some of the highest absolute and relative pre-transfer, and the highest post-transfer, poverty rates in the developed world.

Overall, the U.S. ranks 16th on the Human Poverty Index. (source: Wikipedia)

Certainly, it would seem with so great a concentration of wealth, poverty would not be an issue. However, statistically speaking, the average yearly median income of households in the U.S. in 2006 was $48,201.00 according to the US Census Bureau. The median income per household member (including all working and non-working members above the age of 14) was $26,036 in 2006.

In 2005, there were approximately 113,146,000 households in the United States. 19.01% of all households had annual incomes exceeding $100,000, 12.7% fell below the federal poverty threshold and the bottom 20% earned less than $20,032. (source: Wikipedia)

As mentioned in Chapter III, with the downward spiral of the economy, enlistment in the military is up. This means young men and women are making 2-6 year contractual obligations whereby they faithfully promise to defend this country, even with the ultimate sacrifice – their life if necessary.

Typical Oath of Enlistment

"I John Paul Jones (your full name) do solemnly swear (or affirm) that I will support and defend the Constitution of the United States against all enemies – foreign and domestic. That I will bear true faith and allegiance to the same. That I will obey the orders of the President of the United States, and orders of the officers appointed over me. According to regulations and the Uniform Code of Military Justice, so help me God. I swear (or affirm) that I am

----

fully aware and fully understand the conditions under which I am enlisting."

Tours of 18-24 months of duty in Iraq and Afghanistan with 6 months respite, and then another 18-24 month tour are becoming commonplace. Imagine the stress and pressure our military men and women are facing personally, in relationships, and as they integrate back into society.

Post Traumatic Stress Disorder (P.T.S.D.) (mentioned in Chapter III, page 51), is an anxiety disorder associated with serious traumatic events and characterized by such symptoms as survivor guilt, reliving the trauma in dreams, numbness and lack of involvement with reality, or recurrent thoughts and images. As the wars continue in Iraq and Afghanistan, PTSD is become more and more pronounced.

Although special counseling centers have been established overseas and in the U.S., in April 2008, Dr. Ira Katz, the Veterans Administration head of Mental Health, admitted they had not reported the high suicide attempt rate among their veterans, 1,000 per month.

Is this another sign that our young men (menservants), young women (maidservants) are simply numbers in a system that keeps the useful and discards the worn out?

This poem is a dedicated in honor to men and women of the Armed Forces, past and present. We remember your sacrifice; your labor is not in vain!

My Country, My Life, My Choice

(by James Langston)

I never considered myself a patriot,

I was a face in the crowd,

Someone who simply went along,

To get along.

Yet, as I raised my hands,

And faithfully pledged,

To serve my country,

The ashen faces of September 11, 2001,

Reminded me, "Without Sacrifice,

There are no Freedoms."

As I crawled on the ground,

With bullets zinging over my head,

Or we rushed the strongholds,

Of suspected terrorist,

I felt my heart pumping,

My thoughts racing,

Wondering, always wondering,

"Does anyone care?"

"Is my sacrifice in vain?"

Suddenly, a bright flash, then silence,

In the blackness of night the chilling words ring out,

"Time of death 20:59."
Somewhere between life and death,
I somehow recalled verses,
That I had learned in Sunday School,

". . . *freely you have received,"*
"Freely you are to give,"
"Great love lays down his life,
"For his friends."

With those words ringing in my soul,
I silently slip into eternity,
As they gather my lifeless remains,
One dear soldier remarks,
"Another hero is headed home."

(Chapter VIII)

And ye shall cry out

because of your King,

and the Lord will not hear

you in that Day

The quote, "Focusing your life solely on making a buck shows a poverty of ambition. It asks too little of yourself. And it will leave you unfulfilled," should serve as a constant reminder of our insatiable quest for fame, success and riches.

As each generation continues this spiraling path, we are drawn further and further from the foundational truths our forefathers sought to engrain in our nation.

Sadly, the name "God" is seldom brought into our conversation without a negative connotation or at the beginning or end of a curse word. If our only understanding of God is as a personal good luck charm, or a glorified bellhop, then we should not be overly disappointed when we arrogantly "snap" our fingers and He does not show up.

Anytime we say we love the Lord, this statement should encompass all that we are and hope to be (including our past, present and future).

In the book of Jeremiah we read, *"For I know the thoughts that I think toward you, saith the Lord, thoughts of peace, and not of evil, to give you an expected end. Then shall ye call upon me, and ye shall go and pray unto me, and I will hearken unto you. And ye shall seek me, and find me, when ye shall search for me with all your heart."*

"And I will be found of you, saith the Lord: and I will turn away your captivity, and I will gather you from all the nations, and from all the places whither I have driven you, saith the Lord; and I will bring you again into the place whence I caused you to be carried away captive" (Jer. 29:11-14).

Today, as never before, we are in desperate need of Biblical direction and leadership. While both presidential candidates promise change, change without Christ as the foundational pillar is only the flip side of a rusty can: one day it too will lose its luster.

When Republican nominee Abraham Lincoln defeated his three opponents in the 1860 election; Northern Democrat branch nominee,

----

Senator Stephen Douglas, Southern proslavery Democrat, John Breckinridge, and the Constitutional Union's, John Bell, he ran on the following Republican platform:

- The central position of the Republicans was opposition to the extension of slavery into the territories.
- Enactment of free-homestead legislation,
- Prompt establishment of a daily mail service,
- A transcontinental railroad and,
- Support of the protective tariff.

Mr. Lincoln stood firm against the issue of slavery in any form or fashion: an issue that would later ignite the country in a civil war. Yet, his courage to do what was right was more important to him than making half-hearted promises for the sake of votes.

The five biggest issues now facing our nation are, 1) the economy/jobs, 2) war in Iraq, 3) health care, 4) terrorism/national security, and 5) ethics/corruption in government (source: ABC News/Washington Post Poll).

If Mr. Obama or Mr. McCain believes they can ameliorate even one of these issues in their short tenure, then a history lesson is in order. The problems of society are a heart problem, not a "lack of this" or "lack of that" problem. We need leadership that will do what is right, not what's popular.

We need a President who will open and close his first session of Congress with a prayer so powerful that the Glory of the Lord will fill the house! I know this is not popular, but it is right!

The 55 framers of the Constitution who gathered at Philadelphia in the spring of 1787 represented an enormous reservoir of practical experience in life and politics.

Thirty-nine of them had sat in Congress, 21 had served in the revolutionary armies, eight had signed the Declaration of Independence, eight had helped to frame state constitutions, and seven had been chief executives of their states. Most important of all, they shared one common characteristic: they were politicians, and the entire framing process was an exercise in the art of democratic political accommodation.

As the days turned into weeks, and no definable draft was completed, tensions and disagreements increased. At one point, the contentions were so strong that it seemed everyone would give up on the idea of a Constitution and create autonomous states. Had this course continued, it would have destroyed the then young United States.

Then, when all hope seemed lost, the elder statesman Benjamin Franklin stood up and addressed this gathering of well-respected leaders.

He said, "In the beginning of the contest with Britain, when we were sensible of danger, we had daily prayers in this room for Divine protection. Our prayers, Sir, were heard, and they were answered. All of us who were engaged in the struggle have observed frequent instances of superintending Providence in our favor.... And have we now forgotten this powerful Friend? Or, do we imagine we no longer need His assistance?"

"I have lived, Sir, a long time, and the longer I live, the more convincing I see of this truth: "that God governs in the affairs of man. And if a sparrow cannot fall to the ground without His notice, is it probable that an empire can rise without His Aid?"

"We have been assured, Sir, in the Sacred Writings that except the Lord build the house, they labor in vain that build it. I firmly believe this. I also believe that, without His concurring Aid, we shall succeed in this political building no better than the builders of Babel; we shall be divided by our little, partial local interests; our projects will be confounded; and we shall become a reproach and a byword to future ages. And what is worse, mankind may hereafter, from this unfortunate instance, despair of establishing government by human wisdom and leave it to chance, war, or conquest."

"I therefore beg to move that, henceforth, prayers imploring the assistance of Heaven and it's blessing on our deliberation be held in this assembly every morning before we proceed to business."

Everyone in the room was moved by Franklin's request. James Madison moved that they follow Franklin's recommendation. Local pastors were called in to lead in prayer at the start of every day.

The result, according to Jonathan Dayton, "We assembled again; and every unfriendly feeling had been expelled, and a spirit of conciliation had been cultivated." Within a relatively short time, the framework was completed for the Constitution, and the first ten amendments, or Bill of Rights! (source: Presidential Prayer Team for Kids)

Our efforts no matter how sincere, without the Lord, blow as the proverbial tumbleweed across the desert – without direction or purpose. "Thus saith the Lord of hosts; The broad walls of Babylon shall be utterly broken, and her high gates shall be burned with fire; and the people shall labour in vain, and the folk in the fire, and they shall be weary" (Jer. 51:58).

In her personal letters, Ms. Agnes (AG-ness) Gonxha (GOHN-jay) Bojaxhiu (boh-yah-JOO) --Mother Teresa-- failed to understand why her labor and works did not bring her into a closer relationship with the One she knew as God.

Although perpetually cheery in public, the Teresa of the letters lived in a state of deep and abiding spiritual pain.

In more than 40 communications, many of which have never before been published, she bemoans the "dryness," "darkness," "loneliness" and "torture" she is undergoing. She compares the experience to hell and at one point says it has driven her to doubt the existence of heaven and even of God. (source: David Van Biema, Time CNN)

Quotes from Theopulus Katrina's letters: (source: "Mother Teresa: Come Be My Light")

- "[But] as for me, the silence and the emptiness is Mother Teresa: Come Be My Light so great, that I look and do not see, — Listen and do not hear — the tongue moves [in prayer] but does not speak ... I want you to pray for me — that I let Him have [a] free

----

hand."

- "The smile is "a mask" or "a cloak that covers everything.""
- "I spoke as if my very heart was in love with God — tender, personal love." "If you were [there], you would have said, 'What hypocrisy.'"

As millions also search for answers, a move to capture the supposed "good" that is in all of us is birthing itself over the nation and world.

This in spite of Isaiah's stern warning, "But we are all as an unclean thing, and all our righteousnesses are as filthy rags; and we all do fade as a leaf; and our iniquities, like the wind, have taken us away. And there is none that calleth upon thy name, that stirreth up himself to take hold of thee: for thou hast hid thy face from us, and hast consumed us, because of our iniquities" (Isa. 64:6, 7).

Oprah Winfrey is pulling out all the stops on her XM Satellite Radio program as she offers a yearlong course on the New Age teachings of, "A Course in Miracles," throughout 2008. A lesson a day will completely cover the 365 lessons from the Course in Miracles "Workbook."

For example, Lesson #29 asks you to go through your day affirming that "God is in everything I see." Lesson #61 tells each person to repeat the affirmation "I am the light of the world." Lesson #70 teaches the student to say and believe "My salvation comes from me."

By the end of the year, "Oprah and Friends" listeners will have

----

completed all of the lessons laid out in the Course in Miracles Workbook. Those who finish the Course will have a wholly redefined spiritual mindset—a New Age worldview that includes the belief that there is no sin, no evil, no devil, and that God is "in" everyone and everything.

A Course in Miracles teaches its students to rethink everything they believe about God and life. The course workbook bluntly states: "This is a course in mind training" and is dedicated to "thought reversal."

The lessons are designed to "unblock the awareness of love's presence" and open up all the power and joy of a deeper awareness in your life. (source: Warren Smith – Herescope)

Quotes from A Course in Miracles,

"There is no sin. . . "

A "slain Christ has no meaning."

"The journey to the Cross should be the last 'useless journey.'"

"Do not make the pathetic error of 'clinging to the old rugged Cross.'"

"The Name of Jesus Christ as such is but a symbol. . . . It is a symbol that is safely used as a replacement for the many names of all the gods to which you pray."

"God is in everything I see."

"The recognition of God is the recognition of yourself."

"The oneness of the Creator and the creation is your wholeness,

----

your sanity and your limitless power."

"The Atonement is the final lesson he [man] need learn, for it teaches him that, never having sinned, he has no need of salvation."

Is it any wonder that our reality is being reshaped, redefined and reduced to a mere thought or emotion?

Someone once said if a tale is heard at least 10 times, those hearing it would more than likely become interested. A hundred times and they will adapt the tale to fit their life. However, if it is heard a thousand or more times, then this idea, thought or perception now becomes their reality.

Through the mediums (i.e., radio, television, newspapers, etc.) the message of "the god within us" is played and replayed over 100,000 times daily. And, sadly, this warped truth is shaping our nation, our economy and now our lives.

Yet, our greatest inequity continues to be our failure to adhere to the law of God. We want the blessings, but care little or nothing for the Giver of the blessings or the change this New Life brings.

Before our spiritual clock of mercy runs out, we need to return to the foundational pillars of our heritage, "In God We Trust."

David in the 51st Psalm gave us the proper attitude of repentance: may we also adopt and embrace this same spirit of humility:

"Have mercy upon me, O God, according to thy lovingkindness: according unto the multitude of thy tender mercies blot out my

----

transgressions.   Wash me thoroughly from mine iniquity, and cleanse me from my sin."

"For I acknowledge my transgressions: and my sin is ever before me. Against thee, thee only, have I sinned, and done this evil in thy sight: that thou mightest be justified when thou speakest, and be clear when thou judgest" (Psa. 51:1-4).

(Chapter IX)

Nevertheless, the People refused
to obey the voice of Samuel

If truth was arbitrary and could be moved an inch each day, by the end of the year, that same truth would be approximately 365 inches or 30.41 feet from its starting point. Yet, the move was so unnoticeable that this new vantage point seems as reliable and as safe as it did a year ago.

On a relative field, this repositioning would be welcomed and whole-heartedly embraced; however, if you are the one walking through a minefield, life and death is measured in preciseness not guesstimates.

In 1909, the National Board of Review of Motion Pictures came

----

into being. Its purpose was to endorse films of merit and champion the new "art of the people," which was even then transforming America's cultural life.

In an effort to avoid governmental censorship of films, the National Board became the unofficial clearinghouse for new movies. In essence they took the responsibility out of the hands of society and told us, "Trust me; I will make these decisions for you."

You can argue that everyone knows movies are only a depiction of life and they have no real influence on the attitudes, decisions or direction taken by society as a whole.

However, tell that to the relatives of the victims murdered by these men. Law enforcement psychologists say each one was simply role-playing characters or scenes from the movie.

- San Francisco – Vadim Mieseges: In San Francisco in April 2000, Mieseges, 27, killed and dismembered his landlord, Ella Wong, 47. **—influenced by the movie, "The Matrix"**
- Montreal – Kimveer Gill: Canadian murderer who perpetrated the Dawson College shooting at Dawson College in Westmount, Quebec, Canada on September 13, 2006. He killed one student and wounded nineteen others before he committed suicide. **—influenced by the movie, "Natural Born Killers"**
- Washington, D.C. – John Hinkley Jr.: Attempted to assassinate U.S. President Ronald Reagan in Washington, D.C., on March 30, 1981, as the culmination of an effort to impress actress Jodie Foster. **—influenced by the movie, "Taxi Driver"**

• Alaska – Robert Hansen: An American serial killer. Between 1980 and 1983, Hansen murdered between 17 and 21 persons near Anchorage, Alaska. —influenced by the movie, "A Game of Death"

The line between right and wrong has been skewed by the movie industry (whether purposely or not) to such a degree that scenes of death, mayhem and destruction are often seen as surreal.

As scene after scene unfolds glamorizing violence; drugs and alcohol, the minds of millions are slowly reprogrammed where these actions are now accepted as "normal."

Although the correlation between the violence in movies and these acts being carried out in society is undeniable, the allurement of riches has made these scenes a necessity if the movie is to sell at the box office.

Ten all-time most violent movies, (source: Film School Rejects)

#1 **Texas Chain Saw Massacre**

#2 **Hostel**

#3 **High Tension**

#4 **The Last House on the Left**

#5 **Spit on Your Grave**

#6 **Clockwork Orange**

#7 **Saw**

#8 **Cannibal Holocaust**

#9 **Thousand Maniacs**

#10 **The Hills Have Eyes**

You might ask, "Why aren't more Christian movies produced? The answer is simple; money.   Only a handful of independent Christian filmmakers have $1 million dollars to invest.

Four years ago, Mel Gibson invested $40-50 million of his own money to make "The Passion of Christ."   Although it did exceptionally well at box offices ($370 million gross domestic, $610 million worldwide), this is not the norm.

The appetite of our society is "blood," "guts," "sex," "profanity," and "drugs": the more attention given to each, the greater the box office draw.

Sadly, churches, with few exceptions, have failed to contend for the faith once delivered unto the saints. The "fire and brimstone" or "cross" preaching churches are outdated and non-effective – so they say!

Like popular restaurants, churches are popping up all over the land. However, most are simply catering to the whims, peculiarities and idiosyncrasies of our flailing society.

Yet, after society hears these predictable, sugar coated and repetitive messages for 2-3 years, be it "prosperity," "self-improvement," "god-hood," "sinless perfection," "name and claim it," or a hundred other aliases, they simply loose their appeal and allurement.

These are but a few testimonies of those wounded by these false messages:

- "I internalized the certain 'elitist' mentality that largely characterizes many Oneness communities, for we all believed we had a 'truth' possessed by very few others. In our view, we alone were the people who knew the one true God; we alone knew who Jesus truly was; we alone baptized correctly; we alone walked 'worthy' of the Lord; we alone, in a word, were 'saved." **—former member of the United Pentecostal Church International**

- "I think for me and a lot of other people who were perhaps recently converted Christians, they have taken biblical truths, and the twist isn't very great, but they are twisted, all twisted. .. there's something in the application of it - and it's so subtle it's hard to put into words - something in the way they apply it that turns it the wrong way." **—former member of the Community of Jesus**

- "I went with my spiritual difficulties to my colleague overseers, but they laughed my questions away saying I was studying more than they did, I had to trust The Organization and if things were wrong I had to wait for Jehovah, who would change things in time. They also warned me for reading all those books from 'Satan's World'. .. So I resigned as an overseer.

Now I did get some problems. Almost never an overseer abdicated voluntarily. Overseers could be removed for immoral conduct, stealing and such things, but to give up such a position voluntarily? Some members of the congregation thought there had to be something wrong with me. But what? Could it be this or that? So the gossip started." **—former member of the Jehovah's**

Witnesses

• "We were afraid of everything - afraid of sickness, afraid of deviating from God's word, afraid of mortal mind, afraid of the body, afraid of sex, afraid of people, of difference, of strangers, even of love.

In truth, no one could blame all of these fears on (ours) or any religion. .. I see now, however, how much influence our religion had on these fears. Christian Science taught the complete power of divine Love, insisting on the power of Love to heal every mental and physical illness. When no healings came, the language of the religion broke down." **—former member of Christian Science**

We could so foolishly say it's their fault and leave it there. However, it's the obligation of every Christian to extend a helping hand (when possible) to any and all who are wounded by life, and "dying" on the side of the road.

"And Jesus answering said, A certain man went down from Jerusalem to Jericho, and fell among thieves, which stripped him of his raiment, and wounded him, and departed, leaving him half dead."

"And by chance there came down a certain priest that way: and when he saw him, he passed by on the other side. And likewise a Levite, when he was at the place, came and looked on him, and passed by on the other side."

"But a certain Samaritan, as he journeyed, came where he was:

----

and when he saw him, he had compassion on him, And went to him, and bound up his wounds, pouring in oil and wine, and set him on his own beast, and brought him to an inn, and took care of him."

"And on the morrow when he departed, he took out two pence, and gave them to the host, and said unto him, Take care of him; and whatsoever thou spendest more, when I come again, I will repay thee. Which now of these three, thinkest thou, was neighbor unto him that fell among the thieves" (Lk. 10:30-36).

When the story broke regarding the underage marriages and pregnancies at the Fundamentalist Church of Jesus Christ of Latter Day Saints Ranch in San Angelo, Texas, the nation was shocked. "How could this happen?" and "Why hadn't someone said anything?" … were a few of the hundreds of unanswered questions.

Yet, the real question should have been, "Why would intelligent, educated individuals embrace a life of slavery and consider it normal?" Or better yet, "Who failed to tell them this was wrong, society or the church?"

As the church goes, so does society. If the church is silent, then society has no choice but to step in and present their version of what behavior is acceptable and unacceptable.

From the time the twelve tribes of Israel split into a northern (Israel, Ephraim or Samaria) and southern (Judah, Jerusalem or Zion) kingdom, the northern kingdom never had a righteous king. All 19 of their kings were introduced as doing that which was "evil."

The southern   kingdom   on the other hand had 8 good and

----

righteous kings, and 20 evil kings. Remember this, godly leadership brings about change.

"If my people, which are called by my name, shall humble themselves, and pray, and seek my face, and turn from their wicked ways; then will I hear from heaven, and will forgive their sin, and will heal their land" (II Chron. 7:14).

Our nation stands on the periphery of change. We've been given an unparalleled opportunity to embrace the ways of the Lord, individually and collectively!

If we do, we have the Lord's promise to delay and in some instances avert the storm clouds of judgment that are taking place.

Yet, this repentance must not be half-hearted or sporadic. It must extend from the White House down to every Congressman, Senator, governmental leader, doctor, lawyer, mother, father, aunt, uncle and child of understanding.

Read how the judgment intended for Nineveh was averted when there was godly repentance and sorrow,

"And Jonah began to enter into the city a day's journey, and he cried, and said, Yet forty days, and Nineveh shall be overthrown. So the people of Nineveh believed God, and proclaimed a fast, and put on sackcloth, from the greatest of them even to the least of them."

"For word came unto the king of Nineveh, and he arose from his throne, and he laid his robe from him, and covered him with sackcloth, and sat in ashes."

"And he caused it to be proclaimed and published through Nineveh by the decree of the king and his nobles, saying, Let neither man nor beast, herd nor flock, taste any thing: let them not feed, nor drink water:"

"But let man and beast be covered with sackcloth, and cry mightily unto God: yea, let them turn every one from his evil way, and from the violence that is in their hands."

"Who can tell if God will turn and repent, and turn away from his fierce anger, that we perish not? And God saw their works, that they turned from their evil way; and God repented of the evil, that he had said that he would do unto them; and he did it not" (Jon. 3:4-10).

The choice is ours to make. We have the power to choose our destiny. If we accept the way of the Lord, we win. Anything else and we lose. Choose wisely.

"I must work the works of him that sent me, while it is day: the night cometh, when no man can work" (Jn. 9:4).

About the Author

James Langston faithfully served his country for 27 years in the U.S. Navy before retiring in April 2003. He is a husband, a father, a grandfather and senior pastor of the Pilgrim Outreach Ministries.

James is ordained and licensed through World Evangelism Fellowship of Baton Rouge, Louisiana. He is a 1976 graduate of El Campo high school in El Campo, Texas.

James oversees all day-to-day operations and the ministries Really Simple Syndication (RSS) Internet feeds in the United States, Canada, and a myriad of international countries.

He teaches in ministerial workshops, and gives primary leadership to the evangelistic, administrative, global outreach and audio and visual departments of the ministry.

Duty Stations:

√USS Dubuque (LPD-8)

√Naval Telecommunications Center (NTCC) Subic Bay, Republic of the Philippines

√USS Fletcher (DD-992)

√Recruit Training Command, San Diego, California

√Naval Telecommunications Area Master Station (NCTAMS), European Central, Naples, Italy

√Service School Command, Radioman "A" Communications School, San Diego, California

Awards: NATO Medal, Navy and Marine Corps Overseas Ribbon, Navy Sea Service Deployment Ribbon, Humanitarian Service Medal, Armed Forces Service Medal, Navy Good Conduct Medal, Navy Meritorious Unit Commendation, Navy and Marine Corps Achievement Medal, Navy & Marine Corps Commendation Medal

In addition to *And the People Cried, 'Give Us A King!'* he has authored *"GrandMamma's Prayers," "The Building of a Church," "The Will to Succeed," "Okay, I'm Saved, Now What?" "Out of the Ashes," "34 Years and Still in Love," "The Wages of Sin," "You Reap What You Sow," "Real Answers to Life's Tough Questions,"* and *"America in Crisis."*

James and his wife Cecilia have been married for more than 36 years and have six children and thirteen grandchildren. They live overseas in Italy.